Understanding Dep

Overcoming Despair Through Christ

Workbook

By Donald G. Miles, Ed.D.

Communications should be addressed to:
Turning Point Ministries, Inc.
P. O. Box 22127
Chattanooga, TN 37422-2127

Scripture taken from the *Holy Bible, New International Version*.® Copyright ©1972, 1978, 1984 by International Bible Society. Used by permission of Zondervan Publishing House.

Extracts from the Insight Group are reproduced by permission of Turning Point Ministries, Inc.

ISBN 1-58119-017-4

Cover Photo by Bob Keebler

About the Author

Dr. Miles is senior pastor at 900-member St. John's Lutheran Church in Denver, Colorado, where he has been since 1991. He leads a multiple staff ministry seeking to change from a more traditional ministry to an outreach to persons without a Lutheran background. Small group ministry, emphasizing cell groups based on the Turning Point model of group ministry, is emphasized. Prior to coming to Denver, he was senior pastor for 10 years at St. John Lutheran Church in Glendale, Queens, New York. During his tenure in New York, the congregation tripled in size, entering fully into a renewal in the Holy Spirit.

Don's first call out of seminary was to the congregation in Queens. Prior to that time, he had a 20-year career in mental health, having been deputy commissioner for Mental Health in New York State at the time he went to Concordia Seminary, St. Louis. He also was superintendent of the Georgia Mental Health Institute in Atlanta and clinical professor of psychiatry at Emory University. His academic background includes a bachelor's and master's degree in psychology and a doctoral degree in counseling.

Understanding Depression Group
Overcoming Despair Through Christ

Contents

Introduction
To Understanding Depression Group

Welcome to the Turning Point small group entitled *Understanding Depression*. This group is for people who are experiencing depression and/or those who want to help someone close to them who is struggling with depression. Our goal is to help people overcome despair through Jesus Christ.

Most life-controlling problems are the "sin that so easily entangles" experienced by every believer, referred to in Hebrews 12:1. They begin as enticements, then comes experimentation, finally drifting into deeper entanglements which can actually change the brain chemistry laying down chemical traces which become part of the addictive process.

Depression, however, is likely to work a reverse pathway. It may begin, for many, with a biological abnormality, often a genetically transmitted defect in which a biochemical predisposition is already present. This form of depression is generally referred to as Major Depressive Disorder (MDD) though it can range from mild to extremely severe. Also, milder forms of depression which have continued without a break for two or more years are generally diagnosed as dysthymia. It is generally understood that dysthymia is also typically a biological disorder. Dysthymia and MDD are so painful they always lead to certain coping mechanisms which become the life-controlling problems for which this *Understanding Depression* group is designed. Bipolar disorders, sometimes called manic-depressive disorders, are also biologically based problems; and some people suffering from them will also benefit from participation in this group. As the name implies, people with a bipolar disorder generally cycle from "highs" to "lows."

The biological basis of most on-going depression.

For most people, all of these depressions are clearly partly biological illnesses although popular opinion still holds that they are entirely psychological disorders and, among some Christians, that they are entirely spiritual disorders. To complicate things further, the biological causes of depression are often misdiagnosed. For example, a frequently overlooked cause of depression is medication prescribed for other purposes. Blood pressure medicines, corticosteroids and other hormones, anti-Parkinson drugs, antianxiety drugs, and birth control pills all affect some people by creating true biochemical depressions. In addition, there are many common physical illnesses which can cause depression in some people, such as:

AIDS
Influenza
Anemia
Lupus
Asthma
Malnutrition
Cancer
Multiple sclerosis
Porphyria
Uremia
Congestive heart failure
PMS
Diabetes
Rheumatoid arthritis
Syphilis
Ulcerative colitis
Hypothyroidism
Infectious hepatitis
Chronic infections (mononucleosis, TB)
Electrolyte imbalance—(including Addison's disease).

Due to the relatively high frequency of these illnesses, especially hypothyroidism, a person with depression should always seek a complete physical checkup, clearly informing the physician that he or she is experiencing a depression and wishes to rule out these types of physical causes. It might be useful particularly to discuss a blood test for thyroid stimulating hormone (TSH test).

There is yet another sense in which depression is a physical illness. As previously mentioned, research indicates there is clearly a genetic element for many. Mental health professionals are not in agreement as to the extent of the genetic influence. Some even deny it entirely despite extensive research evidence for a genetic factor. Dr. Arthur Falek, head of the Human Genetics Laboratory at the Georgia Mental Health Institute in Atlanta, once explained that he was perplexed at the never-ending debate between mental health professionals over the "nature vs. nurture" issue; that is, whether people experience various problems because of their heredity or because of their life experiences. "Can't they ever get it straight," he said, "that every human being is in every aspect a product of both?"

Applied to depression, Dr. Falek's observation would contend that every depressed person experiences this disorder in some ways determined by heredity and biology and in other ways determined by life experiences. The mix may vary from person to person, but both are involved in the shape and extent of the problem. From the Christian perspective, Scripture appears not only to endorse Dr. Falek's two-factor hypothesis, but adds a third: the spiritual dimension.

The Apostle Paul writes a benediction to the Thessalonian believers in which he prays, "May the God who gives us peace make you holy in every way and keep your whole being—spirit, soul (Greek: psyche), and body—free from every fault at the coming of our Lord Jesus Christ"(1 Thessalonians 5:23 *Today's English Version*). Secular mental health professionals will almost always ignore the spiritual dimension of human life in their intervention methods and, thus, do not care for the "whole being." The great strength of the *Understanding Depression* group is its full attention to this dimension of human life. In fact, the spiritual aspect may be the most significant determinant of ultimate outcome in regard to coping with severe depressions. Nevertheless, the same caution Dr. Falek gives to the secular practitioner is valid for the Christian—depression is always a mix of spiritual, psychological, and physical elements. To declare depression to be an entirely spiritual problem is both unscriptural and unwise as is the secular tendency to declare it entirely a biological or entirely a psychological problem.

What sort of psychological intervention should be made?

Our society has come to highly value something generally called *therapy*, meaning *psychotherapy*. It is usually associated with persons with special academic qualifications such as a Ph.D., MSW, M.D., etc. Both in secular and in Christian circles, training and credentialing have come to be prized, and warnings of danger are issued from all quarters concerning counseling by nonprofessionals. Research on the question of therapy with people suffering from depression supports the previous argument for multiple causality and shows that the best results come from treating such persons both psychologically and biologically. However, there is no published research indicating what further gains may be enjoyed when the spiritual dimension of life is also added to the treatment of depression.

The power of faith in Jesus Christ will, however, manifest itself in your work with this *Understanding Depression* group. Research published to date does show that it makes no difference what professional degree the therapist has, the outcome apparently being more dependent on certain individual factors in the therapist. Little research has been done on the issue of whether or not professional training itself is of value although some studies seem to indicate that so-called *lay counseling* may produce the same or even better results as that achieved by professionals. It would appear, again, that the individual characteristics of the counselor may be the primary determinant of effectiveness. Some of the issues surrounding the place of

professional therapy for Christians are addressed with sophistication in the recent writings of Dr. Larry Crabb, a Christian clinical psychologist. This depression group deals only with Christian, spiritual healing and support for depressed persons. This rather lengthy discussion of the psychological and physical elements of depression is given simply so that you will be aware of the nature of this disorder and can urge your group members also to be aware that they will need to consider simultaneously adding biological (medical/psychiatric) and psychological support to their lives. Since the group itself will offer considerable psychological support, many participants may choose to postpone or ignore entering into *therapy*. However, it would be wise to caution those who do to choose someone who is not in conflict with the biblical/spiritual content of the *Understanding Depression* group.

What is the role of antidepressant medication in depression?

Because of the research showing that medication is effective for most—estimates are between 50 and 80 percent—it would be best for participants to explore obtaining a prescription from their family physicians if not from a psychiatrist.

Most antidepressants today are prescribed by family doctors, not psychiatrists. Ordinarily, they have sufficient training and experience to manage the type and dosage levels for many people without difficulty. In drug resistant or non-responsive cases or where there are troublesome side effects, it is often wise to consult a psychiatrist.

There are several types of antidepressant medications now available and several more under development and/or FDA review. Finding the right medication at the right dosage with minimal side effects is sometimes a two- to six-month process of trial and error. Further, both general practitioners and psychiatrists have great variability in attitudes and experience in prescribing antidepressants. It is therefore often wise to do one's own reading or consult someone for a second opinion. The University of Maryland Department of Pharmacology has an internet service called PharmInforNet meant to aid users with unanswered medical/pharmaceutical questions about antidepressants. Their address is http://www.pharmacy.ab.umd.edu/

What does depression look like?

This group is not intended for situational (reactive) depression. It is to be noted first of all that this group is for those persons with depressions that only partially involve current life trauma. Those who are depressed as a result of personal loss, such as death or divorce, have situational (reactive) depression. Situational depressions are those normal depressions which come into the lives of all human beings. Living in a broken, sin-filled world will lead to many betrayals, sicknesses, and losses which are deeply depressing. An excellent resource for these depressions is the curriculum, *Handling Grief and Loss* by Dr. Raymond T. Brock, also available

from Turning Point. Because these depressions are reactions to external life events, they usually have a different duration and outcome than do the types of depressions for which the *Understanding Depression* group is intended.

This group is for those whose depression is of an ongoing nature, perhaps occurring in cycles, and not particularly associated with recent personal losses although for many people with depression, there is a mixture of the two types of depression, i.e., both situational and ongoing. This group is also for those who want to develop a better understanding of depression in order to help their friends and loved ones deal with this struggle.

Ongoing depression, even when there has been a situational, traumatic precipitating event in a person's life, will show most of the symptoms listed below in most people. When in doubt, make a referral to a skilled mental health professional. Unless hostile to Christianity, most mental health professionals will be glad to work cooperatively with a spiritually oriented support ministry. The professional of choice, unless the referral is to a multidisciplinary group practice, will be to a psychiatrist. As a physician, the psychiatrist is able to prescribe antidepressant medication which is, as noted above, of significant importance for a majority of people with depression.

1. A family history of depression or alcoholism. Many counselors are skeptical of the genetic hypothesis for clinical depression. Nevertheless, there is a body of well-conducted re-

search indicating there is indeed such a link. Further, the link seems to indicate the genetic factor responsible for alcoholism is also present in many depressions. For example, one study indicates the daughters of alcoholic fathers have a significantly higher likelihood of experiencing depression than daughters of nonalcoholic fathers while the sons will have a significantly higher incidence of alcoholism. Some of these studies involve following identical twins raised in different environments. Thus the influence of home and family life can be sifted out allowing researchers to understand the biological influence. In a majority of long-standing, major depression disorders, a family history of depression and/or alcoholism will be found somewhere in the family tree.

2. A long-standing cyclical problem. Clinical depression can often be traced back into childhood. People often report they always knew something was different about themselves. Some severe depressions run in cycles, sometimes going for months between the deep valleys, sometimes cycling rapidly, perhaps around the monthly menstrual cycles. People will recognize most of the following symptoms as having been present.

3. Interpersonal relationships are difficult. Emotions are likely to be flattened despite the likelihood of bouts of weeping. The person doubts that he or she knows what love is. There is often a desire to withdraw from social contacts even with members of the immediate family. The difficulty in forming and/or maintaining intimate relationships extends also to

God. He seems distant and un-available to the person with depression.

4. Irritability and anger. One of the factors involved in preventing the formation of intimate relationships is the problem of irritability. Loved ones, co-workers, and even neighbors are likely to notice this. They report having to "walk on eggshells" around the depressed person. It is as if the person with depression has a radar antenna which is constantly scanning the horizon to "lock in" on the cause for the irritability. Psychologically, the person with depression has difficulty tolerating the thought that he or she is just simply irritable and there is little or no external cause. He or she does, however, usually admit they seem to overreact to external events and are often puzzled at why they become so angry over trivial matters.

5. Sleep disorder. Various types of insomnia are common, especially waking up after only two or three hours of sleep and being unable to fall asleep again. For some, the reverse is true—too much sleep. Typically, this occurs after a time of difficulty in first falling asleep, then being unable to get up in the morning. For some working people, there is sleeplessness during the week followed by a weekend consisting of sleeping about 50 percent of the time.

6. A desperate search for the cause. In the search for *the cause* of their depression, people are especially vulnerable to the Freudian speculations of our age. They suspect, often with the encouragement of others, that *the cause* must be something from their childhood. Of course, there often are child-

hood traumas which do influence the depth and course of depression. Nevertheless, in most true depressions, a person's disorder cannot be effectively dealt with using only the psychological pathway. Such persons are especially vulnerable to suggestions of childhood parental abuse and, given the theoretical orientations among some mental health professionals, may be inaccurately diagnosed as victims of childhood sexual abuse or suffering from multiple personality disorder (MPD). The implantation of false memories by some mental health professionals has become something of a national scandal. Recent research on what is called "source amnesia" reveals that once the source of a memory is forgotten, people can confuse an event that was only imagined or suggested with a true one. The result is a memory that, though false, carries the feeling of authenticity. True MPD, if it exists at all, is extremely rare. These comments are not, however, to minimize the actual frequency or seriousness of true childhood sexual abuse and its devastating consequences.

7. A sense of going crazy. During the valley of a depressive cycle, a person is likely to feel right on the edge of losing it. For mothers with young children, there is sometimes a fear of going over the edge and becoming dangerous to the children. This seldom, if ever, happens, but the fear of losing control is very stressful. Sometimes the person with depression is disappointed to learn that their depression is not a mental illness in this sense. This disappointment may be understood as due to the person's desire to gain relief from the pain of de-

pression by simply *going crazy* and not having to continue to experience the enormous daily energy drain and extreme pain of coping with depression.

8. A deep sense of worthlessness. Perhaps the most hurtful symptom of all is the abiding sense of worthlessness. This is so deeply rooted that it often does no good at all for caring family members or other Christians to offer words of encouragement. When all the good things about a depressed person are pointed out, the person will hear it as either false praise or else the words of one who does not really know them. For this reason, it is sometimes a serious mistake to try to "cheer up" a depressed person. Here is the point at which deep spiritual warfare takes place. The devil, the "accuser of the saints," usually plays his "tape" into the mind, with words such as, "You really are a loser. You might fool some people into thinking you are worthwhile, but you will never fool God. He knows you are nothing but junk, and you know that you are junk. Why don't you save everyone a lot of trouble and just kill yourself?"

When the depressed person is also a Christian, it becomes even more depressing to find the mind preoccupied with thoughts of suicide. This is due to the feelings of guilt over such contemplated sin. It is not a useful approach to tell the person all the reasons he or she has to live. This will only be interpreted as words of nonsense, as flattery, or as naiveté.

9. Various physical disorders. These disorders are real and often quite painful. They usually consist of headaches, back-aches, and gastrointestinal disorders. It is not clear as to why these sorts of physical symptoms accompany depression since they are not simply attention-getting devices. The depressed person would love to be free of them, but they do not respond to ordinary medical treatment.

10. Eating disorders. Many depressed persons find themselves eating either too much or too little. Serious weight gain or loss also adds further stress to the person's devalued self-image.

11. Memory problems. A high proportion of depressed persons report having memory problems. Even important appointments and events are forgotten. Without a careful daily, written schedule, it may be difficult to be reliable in meeting routine responsibilities.

12. Energy loss. In the valleys of depression, even routine tasks may become more than available energy can accomplish. Doing the dishes or the laundry, much less going to work or school, are seemingly beyond possibility. Loved ones, co-workers, and others may take it as laziness and become hurtfully critical. Even the depressed person cannot understand it, and the feelings of worthlessness are reinforced. Some people cope with the energy drain by spending their weekends mostly in bed restoring their energy. The energy loss can extend in any direction. A common problem is loss of sexual energy, resulting in reduced receptivity to sex. A mate is likely to experience this as rejection and to respond with hostility, further increasing the isolation of the depressed person.

13. Resistance to antidepressant medication. It is curious that it is almost diagnostic of people with depression that they will ordinarily be resistant to the idea of trying medication. Among Christians, this resistance is often supported by well-meaning radio and television teachers. Because of the negative effect caused by depression on a person's sense of self-worth, the suggestion of medication is often interpreted by the depressed person as a statement to the effect, "You are really quite inadequate and beyond repair. All we can do is give you a pill and push you out of the way. You are sick, and sick people need pills." People usually end up trying medication only after they have tried "gutting it out," "praying it out," or after months of psychological counseling has produced little relief. Even then, they typically quit taking their medication after a month or two even if they have good results simply because they once again feel condemned by the very act of taking a pill. Occasionally, an argument can effectively be made that since they are willing to take an aspirin for a headache or insulin for diabetes, there is no difference in taking an antidepressant for depression. Still, a majority will reject the argument. Only reluctantly and after continued suffering will most depressed persons seek an antidepressant prescription and stick with it for the six months minimum necessary to make a possibly lasting impact on brain chemistry.

Welcome

Personal Notes

Welcome to our *Understanding Depression* group. You have taken a positive step. We thank God for you.

During this course there will be five daily devotions for each session listed after each lesson. Do the daily devotion each day from pages 14 to 17 prior to this group meeting.

Self-Awareness

We're thankful you have joined this group. I know you are curious to know more about just what sort of group it will be.

This group is for people who have struggled with depression, who are tired, hurting, and discouraged about life. It is also for the loved ones of those who are depressed, people who are seeking understanding and help in living with a depressed person. Both Christians and non-Christians are welcome. If you are not yet a believer in Jesus Christ, we want you to know that we—and God—love you very much. In the weeks ahead we will be sharing together the great healing power of God's love in Jesus. For some people, simply inviting Jesus to take up residency in their heart is a deeply healing experience. We believe that God wants all people to know Him and that He is holding out His arms to all of us, but we do not want to pressure anyone to make a commitment to Jesus or, for that matter, to do anything at any time that they do not feel comfortable doing.

What will we do here each week as we begin to deal with depression and its consequences? Here is an idea of what will happen during a typical meting.

First, we will pray together. Prayer is the method by which we are able to reach out to God and praise and thank Him, to take hold of His promises, and to tell Him of the heaviness of our hearts. Then we'll spend a few minutes talking together and getting to know each other better. We don't want to be a circle of strangers. But in saying that, please understand that in any of the group conversations, you should never feel pressured to talk. We only want you to speak when you feel comfortable doing so. We do not want to put you on the spot.

Self-Awareness
Next in each meeting comes something we call our "self-awareness time." This part of the meeting is for the purpose of helping us to understand depression and its consequences better. During this time, we'll discuss some of the practical issues involved in dealing with depression. We'll look at how depression affects our spiritual and emotional well-being.

Spiritual Awareness
After our self-awareness time, we will open our Bibles and spend some time working together on the qualities God wants to build into our lives. If you can picture depression as a downward spiral that has the potential to pull us deeper and deeper into despair, then the qualities we'll study from God's Word are like a ladder that helps us to climb out of this deep hole.

David in the Bible recognized the need to have God as his tower of strength. He said:

> **The LORD is my rock, my fortress and my**
> **deliverer; my God is my rock, in whom**
> **I take refuge, my shield and the horn**
> **of my salvation. He is my stronghold,**
> **my refuge and my Savior (2 Samuel 22:2-3).**

If you are not now in a personal relationship with Jesus or not sure if you are, you may want to use this as your prayer to Jesus.

Dear Jesus,

I deeply regret all the things I have done wrong in my life. (Take a few moments to confess silently the things that are particularly heavy on your conscience.) I ask you to forgive me, and I now turn away from everything I know is wrong.

Thank You for dying for me on the cross so that I can be forgiven and set free from depression and all my other problems. Thank you for being willing to forgive me, not because I deserve it but because I believe in Jesus who died for me. Thank you for the gift of your Spirit who gives me strength to live a new life. I now receive that gift. Come into my life, Lord Jesus, by Your Holy Spirit to be with me forever.

Thank You, Lord Jesus. Amen.

Application

After our weekly Bible study, we'll take some time to work on applying it to our lives. God cares about the pain depression causes, and we will together seek His solutions in our meetings. We will seek to appropriate God's healing, His power to cope with the deep hurts of our hearts, and His life-changing principles for effective living. This will also include an expectation that God answers our weekly prayers together.

Ground Rules

Listed below are some basic ground rules for our *Understanding Depression* group.

1. **We want you to be here.** Make every effort to be here. Make these nine sessions a top priority in your life. Each session is important to you, and you are important to the group. In addition to what God wants to do in your life, you have a great deal to contribute to the lives of others in this group. If you cannot attend for some reason, please give one of us a call to let us know.

2. **You should speak within your own comfort level.** This should be a nonthreatening place. Do not feel pressured to speak.

3. **There is to be confidentiality concerning anything that is shared within the group.** We must be able to trust each other to maintain confidentiality. (I might add here that it is important for us to maintain the confidences of the other people in our lives, too. This is not the place to tell what you know about your spouse's problems or your children's or your friend's. It is not appropriate to gossip.) The only exception to maintaining confidentiality should be when a person is a danger to themselves or to others.

Workbook: *Understanding Depression*, Turning Point, P. O. Box 22127, Chattanooga, TN 37422-2127

4. **Make a commitment to prepare for each session.** Your workbook is a private place—just between you and God. No one else ever needs to read what you have written there. Do take time to let God work in your life during the week as you prepare for our time together in the group.

5. **Spend time alone with God every day.** Included in the workbook are some suggestions for how you might spend approximately 30 minutes a day in Bible reading, meditating on God's Word, and in prayer. That time alone with God could be the most significant element of the healing and the building God wants to do in your life.

   Sometimes depression makes it very difficult to spend more than three or four minutes doing this. If this is true for you, just do what you can. The Bible says, "Therefore, there is now no condemnation for those who are in Christ Jesus" (Romans 8:1). You will find yourself being tempted to believe that God has nothing to say to you and that you are too far gone to be cared for by God and are under His condemnation. But this is simply a satanic attack. Jesus called the devil "the father of lies." The fact that the devil can and does plant serious lies in your mind is a point we will come back to time and again.

6. **Keep in mind that this group is not a substitute for medical or psychological care.** We never advise anyone to stop taking prescribed medications or cancel their doctor's care.

What circumstances led to your being a part of this group? How did you hear about it? What made you think you wanted to be a part of it?

Through the course of our Spiritual-Awareness studies, we are going to look at a lot of different Bible verses, but there is one passage we will focus on and return to again and again.

This is a very special portion of God's Word that gets right to the heart of our struggles with the problems that master us. Please read 2 Peter 1:3-11 and then the paraphrased passage below from *Epistles Now.*

2 Peter 1:3-11

Do we really believe
   that our great God has granted through His
   Spirit everything we need to be happy and
   contributive as His children and servants?
It's true!
But like money in some savings account
   God's precious gifts remain in the bank
   and our lives remain dwarfed and pinched,
   largely dependent upon small talents
   and starved by large doubts.
Only by cashing in on God's glorious promises
   are we able to live effectively
   and productively
   in our kind of world.

There are other things
   we must stir into the divine recipe
   for joyous living in a joyless society.
A large measure of faith must be laced gener-
   ously with kindness and goodness.
Added to that must be an ever-open mind,
   a searching, reaching grasp for truth.
Courage and fortitude,
   a dogged determination to keep going,
   a persistent, day-by-day surrender
   to God and His purposes,
   are necessary for Christian maturity.

Then there must be love–and added to love,
   more love, for this is the most important ingredient of all.
It is this that makes for authentic Christianity.
Without these qualities
   our witness will have little effect
   on the suffering, lonely, loveless, oppressed,
   and indifferent inhabitants of this planet.

We certainly ought to be aware of these things
   that are needed to make our Christian exper-
   ence genuine and permanent.
Nevertheless,
   we need occasional reminders and chal-
   lenges, for, it seems, we are quick to slack off
   when life becomes comfortable or the road
   ahead appears a little easier to negotiate.
This may well be one of the reasons our loving
   God permits suffering to afflict us;
   it keeps our heads straight and our hearts focused on the truly important goal of our
   lives, a right relationship with God.

Workbook: *Understanding Depression*, Turning Point, P. O. Box 22127, Chattanooga, TN 37422-2127

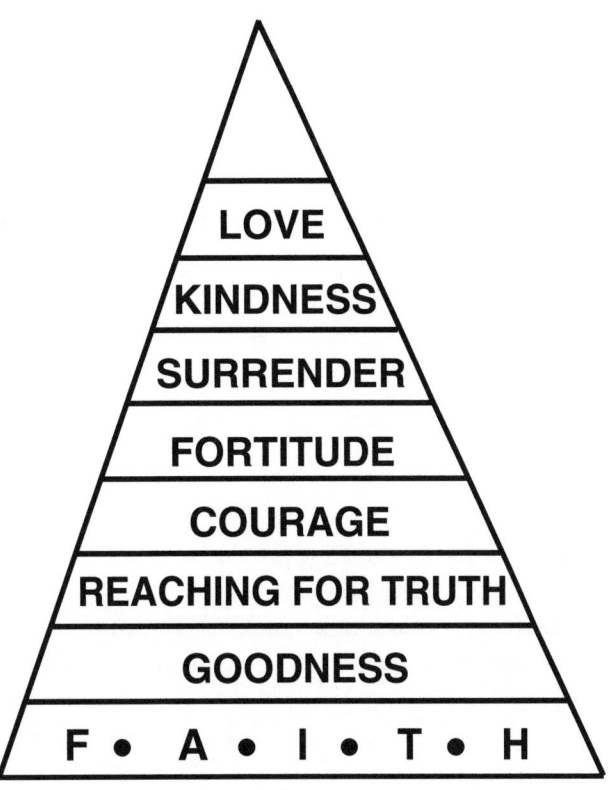

THE UPWARD PATH TO VICTORY OVER DEPRESSION

LOVE

KINDNESS

SURRENDER

FORTITUDE

COURAGE

REACHING FOR TRUTH

GOODNESS

F • A • I • T • H

In the first paragraph of this chapter from 2 Peter, what does it say God has given to us?

What do you think "everything we need" includes?

Does it say that anyone is left out?

Does it say that God "will give" or "might give" us everything we need for life and godliness?

Why do you suppose we often feel that we have *not* been given everything we need for life and godliness?

Let's look now at the remainder of the first part of 2 Peter 1. It says that for many believers, "Like money in some savings account God's precious gifts remain in the bank"! What do you suppose causes us to leave such precious gifts in the bank?

How does it make you feel when you live a "dwarfed and pinched" life? Do you sometimes think that such a life isn't worth living and that the world would be better off without you?

In 1 Corinthians 3:16-17, Paul writes, "Don't you know that you yourselves are God's temple and that God's Spirit lives in you? If anyone destroys God's temple, God will destroy him; for God's temple is sacred, and you are that temple." What do you think this means, especially for yourself?

Workbook: *Understanding Depression*, Turning Point, P. O. Box 22127, Chattanooga, TN 37422-2127

Application

List any questions you may have, either about this session or what we will do in the weeks ahead.

Please read the testimony below.

A Testimony of Encouragement

By Linda Justin

Turning the depression over to God helps me deal with it. I accept the depression. Sometimes I cannot pray more than, "Please help me, O God." At those times God takes over. The Holy Spirit prays for me and ministers to me. It is okay to cry and to withdraw. The Holy Spirit draws me back out later after my soul has been nourished and renewed.

It is not an easy thing to let go and let the Lord do this work. I must trust God absolutely. Depression tells me that I am helpless and hopeless; nothing will ever be okay with my life again; nothing will happen that is good; there is no reason to try. The tears are just below the surface and waiting to spill my sorrow out. I can do nothing but lie there. I find myself lying down nearly all the time, either sleeping or dulled by the depression to the point that I have no desire to leave my bed. I am drained. I have no energy, no capacity to relate to others. It is next to impossible to move my legs to stand up.

While I am thus withdrawn, I do not think about much. I do not feel much. I allow my body and soul to rest in the arms of God. He carries me to the end of the episode and restores my hope and my presence of mind.

There are times I must get up and participate in life during depression; the Holy Spirit keeps me going then, too. When I cannot raise my legs, the Holy Spirit moves them, directing my movements. When I cannot see how I will survive the next minute, the Holy Spirit leads me. When I am shut down; the Holy Spirit opens up a storehouse of grace for me. The Holy Spirit acts for me and carries my load while I rest, no matter how long it takes.

→ **Day One**

Scripture: Read again the first five lines of 2 Peter 1 as printed in the paraphrase in the Guide.

Questions for Meditation:

1.   What does Peter say that you have received through the
     Holy Spirit?

2.   Will you confess that you have received it since God can-
     not lie?

3.   When you read that you have a gift of faith that gives you
     "everything you need to be happy and contributive," what
     comes to mind as you consider your life right now?

4.   Read Hebrews 11:1. Do you have to see or feel the gifts of
     God to know they are true?

Suggestions for Prayer:

1.   Pray again for Jesus to come through the door of your life
     and eat with you.

2.   Thank God for the gift of faith that His Spirit gives you.
     Thank Him for giving you everything you need to make
     your life worthwhile. Let faith, not experience, guide your
     prayer.

3.   Invite the Holy Spirit to fill you again this day.

→ **Day Two**

Scripture: Read Philippians 4:4-9.

Questions for Meditation:

1.   From verse 5, where is the Lord?

2.   How does this help you to stop worrying (verse 6)?

3.   Does God want you to talk to Him about your depression
     and all the concerns in your life (verse 6)?

4.   What does the peace that comes from God do for you
     (verse 7)?

5. Instead of discouraging and pessimistic thoughts, with what is it possible for you to fill your mind?

6. What will happen if you practice Paul's words?

Suggestions for Prayer:

1. Give yourself to the Lord and ask Him to carry your worries.

2. Pray for everything you can think of that is a burden in your life.

3. Pray a prayer of thanksgiving for the blessings in your life. (Yes, there are some!)

4. Pray according to each positive mind-set Paul describes.

↪ **Day Three**

Scripture: Read 2 Peter 1:3-11 again using a regular Bible, not our paraphrased passage.

Questions for Meditation:

1. From verse 2, what is grace? (**G**od's **R**iches **A**t **C**hrist's **E**xpense—a free gift, received by faith)

2. What is true peace? (Review yesterday's devotion.)

3. Do you have "knowledge of God and of Jesus"?

4. If you have doubts, what does Jesus invite you to do? (See item 1 in Day One.)

Suggestions for Prayer:

1. Pray for grace and peace.

2. Pray again for Jesus to enter the door of your life and to eat with you.

3. Pray again for the Spirit's power to strengthen your faith.

→ **Day Four**

Scripture: Read 2 Corinthians 10:3-4.

Questions for Meditation:

1. What is the "war" in your life?

2. What might Paul mean that we do not wage this war as the world does?

3. If we have different weapons, what are they?

4. In what way is attending the Depression Group a weapon?

5. What other weapons does a Christian have?

6. What "strongholds" might the devil have tried to establish in your life?

7. Do these strongholds seem to keep you from the knowledge of God?

Suggestions for Prayer:

1. Pray to God to rebuke Satan who is a defeated foe because of the resurrection of Christ Jesus.

2. Pray for the Spirit's power to wage war on your behalf.

3. Pray against the lie that you are of no worth or value.

4. Pray that your eyes might be opened to see the great value God has placed on you; so much so that He sent His Son to die for you.

→ **Day Five**

Scripture: Read Philippians 1:3-6.

Questions for Meditation:

1. Do you know that there are Christians somewhere giving thanks to God for you?

2. What is it about you (or Christ in you) that gives joy to others when they think of you?

3. Have you considered that because you are a Christian, you are in partnership with other believers in the gospel?

Workbook: *Understanding Depression*, Turning Point, P. O. Box 22127, Chattanooga, TN 37422-2127

4. What does it mean to be in partnership in the gospel?

5. Have you considered that God is at work in you to bring you to completion; that you do not need to do this yourself?

6. What do you suppose you will be like on the day of completion?

Suggestions for Prayer:

1. Because you find joy in seeing others come to Christ and live in Him, perhaps you can do for others (give thanks for them) just as somewhere God has raised up someone to give thanks for you.

2. Pray that the victory which God is at work in you to produce will be a testimony to the gospel in the years ahead.

3. Pray for a fresh infilling of the Holy Spirit who is the power of God to transform you and bring you to completion.

Session 2 Symptoms of Depression

Meet With God

Personal Notes

Do the daily devotion (pages 22 to 25) prior to this group meeting.

Self-Awareness

Read the *Introduction* section which is printed on pages 1-5.

After reading this article, do you think you or your loved one is struggling with depression? If so, how did this make you feel?

Does it help you any as you think about yourself or about your loved one with depression to consider the type and severity of depression as the result of three factors: biology, environment, and spirituality? Can you see all three at work in your life?

Note the 13 symptoms (pages 3-5) which characterize the types of depression for which this group is intended.

Workbook: *Understanding Depression*, Turning Point, P. O. Box 22127, Chattanooga, TN 37422-2127

As we spend time together over the weeks ahead and work on some important issues, it's our desire that we will come to trust each other. We hope you'll come to feel that the group is a "safe place" to express yourself—because we can all trust each other.

Even more important than finding people we can trust is learning to trust God.

What are some ways that trust in God and trust in people are alike?

How are trust in God and trust in people different?

Spiritual-Awareness

Another way to say "trust in God" is to use the word faith. You'll remember that during our first session, we briefly identified eight objectives listed in 2 Peter 1 that will result in God's power taking effect in our daily lives. We listed them in the form of a pyramid because we are going to build these things together into a new life. The foundation level is faith. Turn in your Bible to 2 Peter 1:1 and see to whom Peter is writing.

Whom is Peter addressing here?

Please look at the well-known biblical definition of faith found in Hebrews 11:1. This was one of our daily devotion verses last week.

What does it mean to you that "faith is being sure of what we hope for and certain of what we do not see"?

Since we Christians all come under spiritual attack from the devil, we waiver from time to time about whether or not we truly have faith. Turn to Revelation 3:20. "Here I am! I stand at the door and knock. If anyone hears my voice and opens the door, I will come in and eat with him, and he with me." Stop for a moment and, by prayer, "knock" and ask Jesus to come in to your life. Remember, Jesus has promised if we do this, He will come in and eat with us. Eating a meal together is one of best ways people have of sharing their lives together in a personal relationship, and Jesus says this is how close He wants to be with us.

Why do you think that faith is the first of the
eight objectives in our pyramid of spiritual
growth?

LOVE
KINDNESS
SURRENDER
FORTITUDE
COURAGE
REACHING FOR TRUTH
GOODNESS
F • A • I • T • H

Application

Faith in Christ is the starting point for all the work God wants
to do in our lives in the weeks ahead.

What does faith in Christ means to you personally?

Is your faith in Jesus Christ the foundation of your life?

When have you been able to rest on (put trust in) that foundation?

How has your faith in Christ made a difference in the important areas of your life? In making important decisions? In dealing with problems? What about in the testing and hard times Peter wrote about?

Workbook: *Understanding Depression*, Turning Point, P. O. Box 22127, Chattanooga, TN 37422-2127

A Testimony of Encouragement

By Trish

As far back as I can remember, I have struggled with depression. Growing up, there was little love or affirmation expressed in my family. Searching for love, at 18 I married the first man who showed interest in me. My marriage quickly became a carbon copy of my parents' unhealthy marriage, although it somehow lasted for 12 miserable years. When it ended, I felt like I had been released from prison, and I had a new hope for my future. (I don't want to give the impression that I take divorce lightly, but I believe that a true marriage has to be united by God.)

I began to seek God's will and He brought a wonderful Christian man into my life. I wish I could say that everything was wonderful after Greg and I married, but I brought a lot of baggage into our marriage and it has been a long, difficult process of healing. Looking back, I can see how far the Lord has brought me, but sometimes I focus on how far I still have to go. I have learned that negative thoughts bring negative feelings which can lead to angry words or self-indulgent behavior. I know this trap so well and yet I still get stuck in it. I believe this is why God tells us to 'take every thought captive' (2 Corinthians 10:5).

Medication does help to 'take the edge off' my irrational thinking, but the best cure I have found is prayer. It helps to have someone else pray with me or FOR me when I can't pray myself. Because this is a daily struggle for me, I am trying to form the habit of asking for God's help every morning–before the crisis situation comes. I know that God can heal instantly, but I believe that sometimes His healing is a slower process which allows us to learn through the experience. I believe that He is teaching me to rely on Him because I am so weak. I am clinging tightly to the promise that "He who began a good work in me will bring it to completion until the day of Christ Jesus" (Philippians 1:6).

DAILY DEVOTIONS
Session Two

→ **Day One**

Scripture: Read 1 Corinthians 3:10-17.

Questions for Meditation:

1. Who is the foundation for an effective life?

2. How is the foundation laid?

3. How is the foundation perceived and received?

4. Do you have anyone whom you allow to build into your life? If not, do you know someone you could ask to do so? Might someone in your group serve this purpose in the future?

5. What might it mean to build with gold, silver, or precious stones?

6. What might it mean to build with wood, hay, or straw?

7. What do you think you are building your life with?

8. What difference does it make what you build with?

9. If you don't like what you have built, what is the consequence of simply "tearing down" (destroying) your life?

Suggestions for Prayer:

1. Pray again for Jesus to come in and be the foundation of your life.

2. Pray for a prayer partner to stand alongside you.

3. Pray for the Spirit's power to build only with good materials.

4. Pray that you might see yourself as built of precious things because of the blood of Christ who purchased you on the cross from a life of sin and death.

Workbook: *Understanding Depression*, Turning Point, P. O. Box 22127, Chattanooga, TN 37422-2127

Scripture: Read 2 Corinthians 10:4c-5.

1. What "arguments" do you suppose Paul is referring to when he says that they set themselves up against the knowledge of Christ?

2. Paul says that these arguments are also "pretensions." A "pretense" is ordinarily understood as something that covers over an underlying truth. What is the underlying truth about what we have been given by God (2 Peter 1, our theme Bible passage)? What pretensions do you suspect might need to be "demolished" in your life in order to enter into this truth?

3. To "take captive" our thought life means that it needs to be incarcerated or put in jail. Who is the only jailor powerful enough to take your thoughts captive since you cannot do it yourself?

Suggestions for Prayer:

1. Use the name of Jesus to come against the arguments and pretenses you discovered in your life. Name each one and renounce them in the name of Jesus.

2. Pray for the power of the Holy Spirit to truly give you the ability to give all of the negativity in your thought-life over to Jesus.

3. Pray for the people against whom you discovered you have negative thoughts, people whom you may have used as an excuse for holding onto arguments and pretensions.

↪ **Day Three**

Scripture: Read Philippians 1:3-6.

Questions for Meditation:

1. In verse 6, Paul says he is "confident" that God has begun a good work in you. Keeping in mind the first level or step of our pyramid based on 2 Peter 1, what is the first element of God's good work in you?

2. Whose job is it to carry on this good work in you? Can you do it yourself?

3. When will the work that God has begun in you be completed?

4. In view of your answer to the previous question, does this
    mean there will be no more progress until Jesus comes
    again?

5.   In view of the promise in 2 Peter 1, do you have faith to
    believe that the good work begun in you includes every-
    thing you need for happiness and productiveness?

6.   Should you be discouraged that your life is still "under
    construction"?

Suggestions for Prayer:

1. Ask God to show you what He has already built into your
    faith life. Pray for confidence in this truth.

2. Pray that you can get out of the way and let God build in-
    to your life daily.

3. In the areas of your life that you think God may be partic-
    ularly seeking to build right now, pray that you might co-
    operate with Him and pray that the spirit of doubt and
    fear might be demolished.

→ **Day Four**

Scripture: Read 2 Timothy 1:7.

1. What do you suppose a "spirit of timidity" is? Might you
    sometimes have such a spirit?

2. If timidity and fear do not come from God and are not
    part of His purpose for our lives, where do you suppose
    they comes from?

3. Is God able to deliver us from this spirit?

4. What spirit did God give to us? Is this part of the "every-
    thing you need for happiness and productivity" of the
    promise contained in our theme verse from 2 Peter 1?

5. Take note that the words "self-discipline" in the NIV Bible
    translate from a Greek word that literally means "a saved
    understanding." Other translations call it a "sound
    mind." Do you sometimes doubt the soundness of your
    mind?

Suggestions for Prayer:

1. Pray against a spirit of timidity in the name of Jesus.

     Workbook: *Understanding Depression*, Turning Point, P. O. Box 22127, Chattanooga, TN 37422-2127

2. Pray for a "spirit of power."

3. Pray for a "spirit of love."

4. Pray for a "spirit of self-discipline" (sound mind).

→ **Day Five**

Scripture: Read Romans 12:1-2.

1. Why do you suppose Paul feels so strongly about this that he "urges" us to this surrender of our bodies?

2. How might you go about offering your body?

3. If God has your body, what else does that include?

4. Is this the way you usually worship God?

5. If you don't conform to the world's ways of thinking, what will happen to your mind?

6. How you ever wondered how to know God's will? How does Paul say you can do so?

Suggestion for Prayer:

Prayerfully give yourself to God confessing to Him all your fears over trusting your life entirely to Him. Confess also to Him all the ways in which you have been conforming your life to the pattern of this world.

 eet With God

Personal Notes

Do the daily devotion each day (pages 33 to 36) prior to this group meeting.

 elf-Awareness

This session is entitled *The Trap*, and many of us experienced it when we tried to answer the question, "What are some good things about yourself?" Sometimes people in a depression group feel trapped by the question itself. On the one hand, we may feel angry and insulted that anyone would question our "goodness." On the other hand, we may find it hard to believe, deep down, that there are good things about ourselves. We are trapped between a rock and hard place, between a deep desire to be affirmed as "good" and a deep feeling of not being very good at all.

The Apostle Paul declared to the Corinthians that "God made him who had no sin to be sin for us, so that in him we might become the righteousness of God" (2 Corinthians 5:21). Depression causes many of us to reject the free gift of God—a new identity as a good and righteous person.

Astronomers tell us there are swirling whirlpools in the universe with a powerful magnetic pull that does not allow light to escape from within them. Black holes, therefore, cannot be seen, but their existence can be identified by the debris that revolves around them. In the same way, we cannot see into the heart of another person, but we can tell the condition of the heart by observing the things that revolve around that person's life. The following diagram illustrates how this might look in a depressed person's life:

Workbook: *Understanding Depression*, Turning Point, P. O. Box 22127, Chattanooga, TN 37422-2127

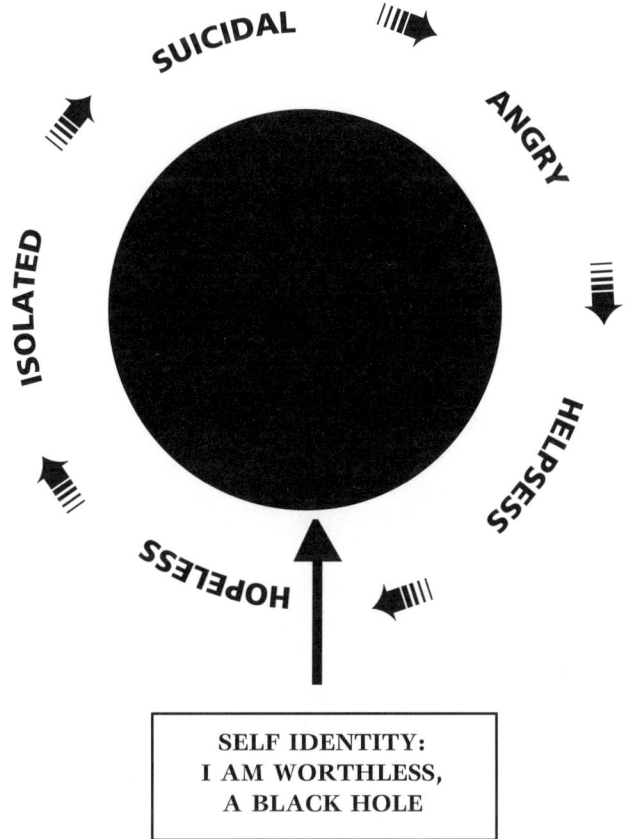

SUICIDAL

ANGRY

ISOLATED

HELPSESS

HOPELESS

SELF IDENTITY:
I AM WORTHLESS,
A BLACK HOLE

The "trap" occurs when we allow our attention to be distracted primarily by the things revolving around our hearts rather than focusing on the condition of the heart itself. For example, anger is one of the primary symptoms of depression, but we can become trapped by our anger when we assume that we are depressed because we are angry rather than that we are angry because we are depressed. This confusion of cause and effect can lead to endless, time-consuming journeys into our childhood experiences in an attempt to find *the cause* of our depression.

As we discussed last week, our childhood experiences do contribute to our present makeup as does our biogenetic and spiritual history. The point is that while our psychological and biogenetic past cannot be changed, our spiritual condition can. If we draw our identity from the negative symptom cluster around us rather than from our true identity as a "new creation in Christ Jesus," then indeed we are continually being sucked into a black hole of despair, and we are easily trapped into a self-reinforcing belief system about ourselves; i.e., "I'm worthless."

In Romans 10 and 11, Paul speaks his heart's desire that his fellow Israelites be saved. These people had a common family history and a common genetic makeup. They had established an identity based on this history with all of its extra-biblical rules developed over the centuries. Out of all of these things, they became entrapped in an identity that would not change even when God offered them a new way of living through faith in their Messiah. To this day, a majority of the Jews have lost out on the promise of God to be a part of the "New Israel." They were trapped into believing that their history of persecution and suffering had to determine their identity rather than that the identity God held out to them would deliver them from their history.

Let's talk about a real life example in which only the name and a few details have been changed to protect this person's privacy. Sandra was a woman in her mid 40s, a highly educated professional woman. One day the bottom fell out of her life, and she entered into a four-year period of major depression. For most of her life she had coped with an underlying depression by detaching herself from real relationships with anyone. As she describes herself, "I was up on a shelf looking down as an outside observer on both myself and everyone else. I couldn't come down and be human and relate to others because the pain would be unbearable. So I did drugs, alcohol, and was sexually promiscuous. Since I felt so worthless, I acted like a worthless person." The energy required to maintain this detachment left Sandra constantly exhausted. She ate obsessively and further despised herself for becoming fat.

Then she broke, no longer able to distance herself from life, and she became almost nonfunctional. She had become a Christian a few years earlier, and now, seething with anger, she went through her Bible from Genesis to Revelation, filling three notepads with angry denials of every promise of God's love, protection, and provision. She also burned with anger at her mother from whom she had never experienced any love or affirmation. There were some indications that she had also been physically and sexually abused in early childhood although she had (and still has) almost no memory of her childhood until about the age of 12. Several counselors, Christian and non-Christian, worked unsuccessfully with her to recover her memories and to forgive her mother. The anger, hopelessness, feelings of worthlessness, suicidal thoughts, inability to work, and overeating preoccupied her. She gave up on herself as did her family and friends. Yet, there was one person, her pastor, who never gave up and constantly told her that with God's help she was going to make it. One day he suggested to her that she read Isaiah 53, personalizing with her own name all the things that the death of the Suffering Servant—a prophetic picture of Jesus—would accomplish for the human race.

So began her healing. Today, about 10 years later, she has a deep sense of her personal worth, is of normal weight, is fully

 Workbook: *Understanding Depression*, Turning Point, P. O. Box 22127, Chattanooga, TN 37422-2127

functioning in her career, and is living a godly life in which she influences many for Jesus Christ. She says her only regret is that there was not a group like this to help her understand her problem was not anger or childhood abuse or even "depression" but rather her self-identity as a worthless person, unloved and unlovable even by God. This identification had come by attending only to the swirling symptoms of depression that surrounded her like the debris around a black hole.

In the weeks ahead, we will carefully seek to learn a new identity, one based on the truth of God's word rather than on a lie from hell. We will return to our theme verses from 2 Peter 1. This new self-identity can also be diagramed. However, like our solar system, the center of the vortex around which the *symptoms* of our lives revolve is composed of light, not the darkness of the black hole.

In our constellation, the sun also attracts a certain type of debris called planets. Light fills this constellation and something called "abundant life" (John 10:10) exists here. The following diagram consists of the way of organizing our lives that we will pursue in the next few weeks. When our lives revolve around a self-identity that is based on faith and formed by the Bible, then we are overcomers of depression.

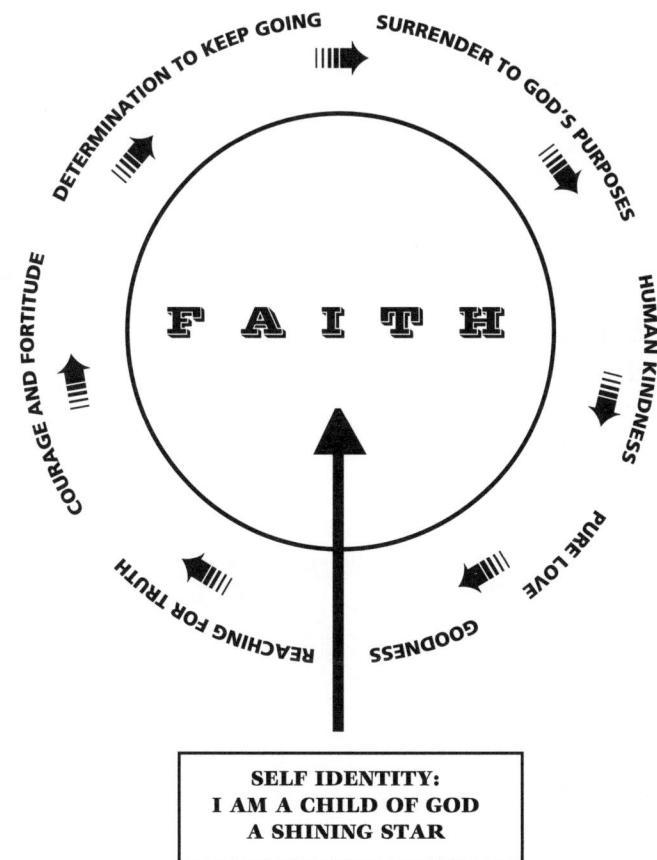

**What do you think of this second diagram? Do you some-
times feel trapped in the first one?**

How do we escape the trap of the first diagram? It can't be
done by willpower. Only the revelation and power of the
Holy Spirit working through our faith can set us free. We may
wonder how our faith can grow and become such a channel
of God's gift of "everything we need." In Romans 10:17(KJV),
Paul writes that "faith cometh by hearing, and hearing by the
word of God." In other words, faith is strengthened as we become a person who is in the Word.

Spiritual-Awareness

For this session, we will begin by looking again at our theme
passage, 2 Peter 1.

Does a Christian already have faith?

**Does Peter say we are lacking something to enable us to have
a real life?**

The more literal NIV Bible translation of 2 Peter 1:4 says that
because we have been given everything we need for happiness
and productivity, we have also received promises from God
that allow us to "participate in the divine nature"!

Does God's own nature revolve around black holes and darkness or around light?

Our paraphrased theme passage tells us that:

> But like money in some savings account
>   God's precious gifts remain in the bank
>   and our lives remain dwarfed and pinched,
>   largely dependent upon small talents
>   and starved by large doubts.

  Workbook: *Understanding Depression*, Turning Point, P. O. Box 22127, Chattanooga, TN 37422-2127

> **Only by cashing in on God's glorious promises**
> **are we able to live effectively**
> **and productively**
> **in our kind of world.**

Peter says there is a common human problem not restricted to people with depression that causes many to live in the black hole of life instead of in the light of God's divine nature. "Only by cashing in on God's glorious promises" do we live effectively and productively. How does one go about "cashing in"? Read Romans 8:12-15.

What does Paul say gives the power to overcome "the misdeeds of the body"?

What do you think it means to "put on the armor of light"?

Our paraphrased theme verse then leads us on, having established that God's Spirit will enable us to add to the faith foundation of our new life in Christ the first ingredient to break forth into light: Goodness. Our theme passage puts it this way:

> **There are other things**
> **we must stir into the divine recipe**
> **for joyous living in a joyless society.**
> **A large measure of faith must be laced generously**
> **with kindness and goodness.**

The key word here in a literal translation is goodness. Other ways to translate this word are valor, excellence, and virtue.

In what ways does depression cause you to lose sight of goodness in your life?

Read Ephesians 5:8-9. Why do you suppose Paul calls goodness a "fruit of the light"?

Read Romans 15:14. Are you as convinced as Paul was that you are "full of goodness"? Further, are you also convinced that you are "complete in knowledge and competent to instruct one another"?

There are three things that will make it hard to apply these biblical truths:

- The biochemistry of our bodies predisposes our minds and emotions to disbelieve that the faith foundation has been laid in our lives so that we can "put on" a goodness which has already been given to us, like a new gift coat.

- Our sin nature, encouraged by our biochemistry, seeks to draw us back into a self-centered life in which goodness seems irrelevant or something that only works for other Christians causing us to isolate ourselves from other relationships.

- The devil desires to keep us from a full realization of who we are in Christ Jesus.

In view of these things, what might you do this week to get a breakthrough on each front?

A TESTIMONY IN POETRY

By Monica Defrancesco

Worth

Oh God,
> You give me value and worth.
> I cannot obtain it from the things that I do.
> I surrender my self-efforts.
> In vain I struggle and strive.
> So Lord,
> I give You my emptiness
>> and receive Your fullness of Spirit.
> I give you my loneliness
>> and believe You are present with me.
> I give you my fears and inadequacies
>> and receive Your unconditional love.
> I give You my worries, doubts, and confusion
>> and receive Your peace.
> I give You my frustrations
>> and receive Your joy.
> I confess and give You my sins
>> and receive Your forgiveness.
> I give You my feelings of worthlessness
>> and believe I am worthy
> Because of Your Son.

→ **Day One**

Scripture: Read Isaiah 53:1-3.

Today we focus on our Suffering Messiah, Jesus, as Isaiah
knew Him in the Old Testament. If living in the light is a
direct result of His suffering, death, and resurrection,
then we can feed our souls the truth that sets us free.

Questions for Meditation:

1. What is the problem with the message of Jesus? Do you
    suppose it is not that what Jesus did for the world is ineffec-
    tive but rather that most people won't believe it? If we
    don't receive the next six verses by faith, then might they
    be ineffective in our lives too?

2. The Apostle Paul says that Jesus came as the second Adam.
    The word "Adam" means "mankind." Jesus came as a repre-
    sentative of the human race to live the perfect life the first
    Adam failed to live and to take upon Himself the punish-
    ment for the sins of Adam and all his descendants, includ-
    ing yours. How does verse 2 describe this man who ex-
    changed His life for ours? Was He much better looking
    than we are?

3. As you read verse 3, do you think Jesus sounds anything
    like us? Why was it necessary for Him to experience this?
    Do you think He is, therefore, able to understand your suf-
    fering?

Suggestions for Prayer:

1. The disciples of Jesus spoke with Him about their doubts
    and areas of unbelief. Talk with Him about yours.

2. Pray about the times you are simply not attracted to be a
    follower of Jesus just as many were when Jesus walked the
    earth. Be open with God about your failures. He already
    knows them and loves you anyway!

3. Tell God about your own hurts and sorrows. Pour your
    heart out to Him. Indeed, if you are able, weep before
    Him. Jesus also wept before God.

Scripture: Read Isaiah 53:4-6.

Questions for Meditation:

1. In the first part of verse 4, the word translated "sorrows" also means pain. In what way did Jesus take up your infirmities and pain? If He took them, why do you hold on to them?

2. The last half of verse 4 says that we humans assume God sent Jesus to the cross. Why do we like to avoid the problem of our own sin?

3. Verse 5 tells us who really was the cause of His being stricken. Who was it? Why, then, did He die for you anyway? Why do you make of the statement that His death was to bring us peace?

4. Verse 6 says that all of us have gone astray. Did this keep Jesus from dying for us anyway? Are you still guilty of anything if God placed on Him the punishment for everything you ever did?

Suggestion for Prayer:

Use your prayer time today as a time of confession, pouring out your heart to God. Remember the promise in 1 John 1:9, "If we confess our sins, he is faithful and just and will forgive us our sins and purify us from all unrighteousness."

→ **Day Three**

Scripture: Read Isaiah 53:7-8.

Questions for Meditation:

1. As you read in verse 7, Jesus went to the cross without a murmur or complaint. Why did He not call on the holy angels to help Him? Why did an innocent man go so quietly to His death?

2. Verse 8 says He was oppressed and judged falsely. Though He was fully human and experienced pain just as you do, God allowed Him no marriage and no descendants. Do you think He was ever depressed?

3. The last half of verse 8 says He was cut off from the land of the living. Is there a difference between giving your life for others and taking your own life?

Suggestions for Prayer:

1. Pray about the example Jesus gave in suffering and what it might have to do with you.

2. Thank God for sending His Son to pay such a price for you in that He was willing to go to the cross so that you might have a new life, receiving through His Spirit everything you need to be happy and productive.

3. Thank God for the pattern in Jesus' life in which suffering leads to death which leads to resurrection. Thank Him for the suffering in your life which now makes you utterly dependent on the Father for resurrection into a new life.

→ **Day Four**

Scripture: Read Isaiah 53:9-10.

Questions for Meditation:

1. Verse 9 goes on to describe what would happen to Jesus after He was "led like a lamb to the slaughter." He was prepared for the grave by hanging on a cross between two wicked men who deserved to die for their crimes/sins. Yet Luke's gospel (23:43) tells us that one of them cried out for mercy, having no time to do any good thing except to believe. Jesus' famous words then crossed the space between their two crosses: "Today you will be with me in paradise." Is there then hope for you? Could Jesus possibly love you as much as this unknown criminal hanging next to Him?

2. Verse 10 tells us it was the Lord's will to crush Jesus and cause Him to suffer. The word translated "suffer" also means weak, sick, and afflicted. Why would it be God's will to do this to His one and only innocent Son?

3. Jesus' death on the cross has been accurately described as a substitute; that is, he took our place, receiving the crushing and suffering that we deserve and substituting His own goodness into our lives. As you think about goodness, how does it make you feel to consider that when Christ died on the cross, His goodness was transmitted to you?

4. The last part of verse 10 speaks of Jesus' offspring—spiritual descendants, including us—and says that the will of the Lord will prosper in His hand. What do you think is God's will for you? Could it possibly be to harm you?

Suggestion for Prayer:

In view of the above Bible verses, your prayer time today might well be best spent in a time of praise and thanksgiving. Think of all the things you dislike in your life and then thank and praise God for nailing them all to a cross so that you might be free to live in the light.

Workbook: *Understanding Depression*, Turning Point, P. O. Box 22127, Chattanooga, TN 37422-2127

Session 4 *Feelings*

Meet With God

Personal Notes

Do the daily devotion each day (pages 44 to 46) prior to this
group meeting.

Self-Awareness

God designed us in His own image as creatures with feelings
and emotions. We read in the Scripture of God's having such
feelings as love, anger, sorrow, and jealousy. Before the fall of
the human race, the original intent seems to have been that
feelings would help us to enjoy the perfection of the things of
God more richly. To be able to only think about things and
not feel them would lead to a barren life; but humanity did
fall, and human emotion has been vulnerable to distortion
ever since. Depression tends to produce its own peculiar pattern of distortion somewhat different than that of people in
general.

On the next page there is a *Feelings Checklist*. Take a minute to
check off the ones that seem more characteristic of yourself.

Feelings Checklist

- ❏ accepted
- ❏ afraid
- ❏ angry
- ❏ anxious
- ❏ attractive
- ❏ beaten
- ❏ brave
- ❏ calm
- ❏ cheated
- ❏ cheerful
- ❏ confident
- ❏ confused
- ❏ cowardly
- ❏ cruel
- ❏ defeated
- ❏ despair
- ❏ desperate
- ❏ different
- ❏ disappointed
- ❏ embarrassed
- ❏ excited
- ❏ fearful
- ❏ forsaken
- ❏ friendless
- ❏ frustrated
- ❏ gentle
- ❏ grateful
- ❏ guilty
- ❏ happy
- ❏ hateful
- ❏ hopeless
- ❏ hurt
- ❏ hypocritical
- ❏ ignored
- ❏ impatient
- ❏ independent
- ❏ inferior
- ❏ insecure
- ❏ jealous
- ❏ judged
- ❏ like a loser
- ❏ lonely
- ❏ loved
- ❏ loving
- ❏ loyal
- ❏ macho
- ❏ misunderstood
- ❏ needy
- ❏ neglected
- ❏ out of touch
- ❏ overlooked
- ❏ persecuted
- ❏ phony
- ❏ preoccupied
- ❏ proud
- ❏ quiet
- ❏ rejected
- ❏ repulsive
- ❏ sad
- ❏ secure
- ❏ shy
- ❏ silly
- ❏ sorry for myself
- ❏ stupid
- ❏ suicidal
- ❏ superior
- ❏ supported
- ❏ suspicious
- ❏ touchy
- ❏ ugly
- ❏ upbeat
- ❏ uptight
- ❏ useless
- ❏ valuable
- ❏ violent
- ❏ weak
- ❏ feelings blocked

Workbook: *Understanding Depression*, Turning Point, P. O. Box 22127, Chattanooga, TN 37422-2127

If you are like most people with depression, you have checked angry, anxious, cheated, despair, friendless, guilty, inferior, judged, like a loser, lonely, misunderstood, repulsive, sad, suicidal, useless, and feelings blocked. You will notice that you have checked very few positive feelings.

Am I right? What do you think about this?

When you try to block your feelings, how successful are you?

Why do you suppose you try to block out the feeling of love in your relationships?

When other people notice how negative and discouraged you feel, how does it make you feel when they try to cheer you up?

Spiritual-Awareness

In this session, we continue to build the pyramid of the "happy and productive" life by adding to faith and goodness, reaching for truth. As our theme passage from 2 Peter 1 puts it:

> **Added to that (goodness) must be an ever-open mind, a searching, reaching grasp for truth.**

The NIV translation of 2 Peter 1:5 puts it more literally: "Make every effort to add to your faith goodness; and to goodness, knowledge."

LOVE
KINDNESS
SURRENDER
FORTITUDE
COURAGE
REACHING FOR TRUTH
GOODNESS
F • A • I • T • H

Reaching for truth or *knowledge* of the truth about the Christian life is an essential for all Christians. Depression adds a dimension of resistance to God's urging of us to reach for truth: Our feelings often do not match up with the truth as revealed in the Bible. Feelings can be more dominant than truth because when they contradict our knowledge of the truth, we experience them as if they were more real. Therefore, before continuing turn to Ephesians 1:18: "I pray also that the eyes of your heart may be enlightened in order that you may know the hope to which he has called you, the riches of his glorious inheritance in the saints."

Since we asked God to give us a heart knowledge of the truth, I believe that He is going to do so. We are going to look at some Bible verses that tell us the truth about ourselves whether we feel it or not and trust that godly feelings will follow truth. Let's begin with the first part of our theme passage:

> **Do we really believe**
> **that our great God has granted through His Spirit**
> **everything we need to be happy and contributive**
> **as His children and servants?**
> **It's true!**

Here we see again that we *have already been granted* everything we need. The last three weeks we have talked about how hard it is to grasp in our hearts that last exclamation: **It's true!**

The following poem was written by a graduate of an *Understanding Depression* group:

Once Again

It's too bad
that so often it seems I forget
what I thought I had learned.
Doubts, insecurities
follow me
showing their faces once again.

Only for me
to once again
choose to believe and walk by faith.

 Workbook: *Understanding Depression*, Turning Point, P. O. Box 22127, Chattanooga, TN 37422-2127

Let's now choose to believe the following verses:

2 Corinthians 5:17
"Therefore, if anyone is in Christ, he is a new creation; the old has gone, the new has come!"

Deuteronomy 1:30-31
"The LORD your God, who is going before you, will fight for you, as he did for you in Egypt, before your very eyes, and in the desert. There you saw how the LORD your God carried you, as a father carries his son, all the way you went until you reached this place."

Isaiah 43:2
"When you pass through the waters, I will be with you; and when you pass through the rivers, they will not sweep over you. When you walk through the fire, you will not be burned; the flames will not set you ablaze."

Isaiah 40:31
"But those who hope in the LORD will renew their strength. They will soar on wings like eagles; they will run and not grow weary, they will walk and not be faint."

Isaiah 41:10
"So do not fear, for I am with you; do not be dismayed, for I am your God. I will strengthen you and help you; I will uphold you with my righteous right hand."

Psalms 147:3
"He heals the brokenhearted and binds up their wounds."

Do these verses say that God's children will never experience hurtful events and feeling? If not, what is the "reach for truth" that they invite you to experience?

Let's look again at the last part of our theme passage:

> **Nevertheless,**
> > **we need occasional reminders and challenges,**
> > **for, it seems, we are quick to slack off**
> > **when life becomes comfortable or the road ahead**
> > **appears a little easier to negotiate.**
> **This may well be one of the reasons our loving God**
> > **permits suffering to afflict us;**
> > **it keeps our heads straight and our hearts focused**
> > **on the truly important goal of our lives,**
> > **a right relationship with God.**

Now let's look at some verses that speak directly to our new identity as children of the light:

Philippians 4:13
"I can do everything through him who gives me strength."

Romans 8:37
"No, in all these things we are more than conquerors through him who loved us."

John 14:12
"I tell you the truth, anyone who has faith in me will do what I have been doing. He will do even greater things than these, because I am going to the Father."

Matthew 5:13
"You are the salt of the earth."

Matthew 5:14
"You are the light of the world."

Luke 12:7
"Indeed, the very hairs of your head are all numbered. Don't be afraid; you are worth more than many sparrows."

John 15:3
"You are already clean because of the word I have spoken to you."

1 Corinthians 12:27
"Now you are the body of Christ, and each one of you is a part of it."

Galatians 3:26
"You are all sons of God through faith in Christ Jesus."

Galatians 4:7
"So you are no longer a slave, but a son; and since you are a son, God has made you also an heir."

Workbook: *Understanding Depression*, Turning Point, P. O. Box 22127, Chattanooga, TN 37422-2127

1 Thessalonians 5:5
"You are all sons of the light and sons of the day. We do not belong to the night or to the darkness."

1 Peter 2:9
"But you are a chosen people, a royal priesthood, a holy nation, a people belonging to God, that you may declare the praises of him who called you out of darkness into his wonderful light."

Matthew 6:26
"Look at the birds of the air; they do not sow or reap or store away in barns, and yet your heavenly Father feeds them. Are you not much more valuable than they?"

2 Corinthians 5:21
"God made him who had no sin to be sin for us, so that in him we might become the righteousness of God."

1 Peter 2:24
"He himself bore our sins in his body on the tree, so that we might die to sins and live for righteousness; by his wounds you have been healed."

Application

Through these Bible verses, we have seen a picture of our new identity in Jesus Christ:

- We are redeemed—paid for at great cost.
- We are forgiven—clean; our sin has been forgotten.
- We are strong and capable—we can do everything through Christ.
- We are conquerors—overcomers.

What does this new identity in Christ mean to you personally?

What would change in your life if you stopped making choices based on your feelings and started living and making decisions based on who you are in Christ?

What struggles can you overcome because of who you are in Christ?

DAILY DEVOTIONS
Session Four

→ **Day One**

Genesis 1:27 — I created you in My image.
Genesis 28:15 — I am with you.
Genesis 49:25 — I bless you.
Genesis 50:20 — I intend good for you.
Exodus 4:31 — I am concerned about you.
Exodus 33:17 — I know you by name.
Leviticus 26:12 — I walk with you.
Deuteronomy 1:30 — I fight for you.
Deuteronomy 1:31 — I carry you as a father carries his child.
Deuteronomy 4:31 — I never abandon you.
Deuteronomy 10:15 — I choose you.
Deuteronomy 32:10 — I guard you as the apple of my eye.
Deuteronomy 33:12 — I carry you upon my shoulders.
Deuteronomy 33:26 — I ride on the heavens to help you.
1 Samuel 12:22 — I am pleased to make you my own.
Psalm 5:12 — I surround you with favor.
Psalm 18:17 — I rescue you.

→ **Day Two**

Psalm 21:2 —I grant you your heart's desire.
Psalm 22:24 — I listen to your cry for help.
Psalm 27:10 — I accept you.
Psalm 33:18 — My eyes are on you.
Psalm 34:18 — I am near you.
Psalm 54:4 — I am your helper.
Psalm 84:11 — I bestow glory on you.
Psalm 91:2 — I am your refuge.
Psalm 100:3 — I am your good shepherd.
Psalm 139:2 — I know your ways.
Psalm 145:8 — I am full of compassion for you.
Psalm 145:15 — I provide for you.
Psalm 149:4 — I take pleasure in you.
Isaiah 40:11 — I gather you in my arms.
Isaiah 41:13 — I hold your right hand.
Isaiah 43:1 — I redeem you.
Isaiah 43:4 — I love you and give you honor.

 Workbook: *Understanding Depression*, Turning Point, P. O. Box 22127, Chattanooga, TN 37422-2127

→ Day Three

Isaiah 43:7 — I deem you precious in my sight.
Isaiah 44:22 — I blot out your transgressions.
Isaiah 46:4 — I carry you even into old age.
Isaiah 49:16 — I have engraved you on the palms of my hands.
Isaiah 54:7 — I will bring you back with deep compassion.
Isaiah 54:8 — I will show you my love forever.
Isaiah 54:13 — I myself will teach you.
Isaiah 57:15 — I revive your spirit.
Isaiah 62:2 — I give you a new name.
Jeremiah 1:5 — I set you apart.
Jeremiah 1:5 — I knew you before I made you in your moth-
              er's womb.
Jeremiah 31:3 — I will love you forever.
Ezekiel 36:26 — I put a new heart within you.
Joel 2:13 — I return to you what has been taken away.
Nahum 1:7 — I care for you.

→ Day Four

Zephaniah 3:17 — I joy over you with singing.
Zechariah 9:16 — I make you to shine as jewels in a crown.
Matthew 6:26 — I consider you most valuable.
Matthew 7:11 — I give you good things.
Matthew 18:12 — I seek after you.
John 3:16 — I give you my only Son.
John 14:18 — I will not leave you as orphans.
John 14:21 — I love you and reveal myself to you.
John 14:27 — I give you my own peace.
John 15:16 — I chose you and appoint you to bear much fruit.
John 17:9 — I pray for you.
Romans 8:1 — I do not condemn you.
Romans 8:14 — My Spirit makes you my child.
Romans 8:22 — All creation awaits my revealing my sons.

→ Day Five

Romans 8:28 — I work all things for your good.
Romans 8:31 — If I am for you, who can be against you?
1 Corinthians 1:9 — I call you into fellowship with me.
2 Corinthians 1:22 — I put my seal on you.
2 Corinthians 2:15 — I make you a sweet savor to me.
2 Corinthians 5:15 — I reconcile you to myself.
2 Corinthians 6:18 — I become a father to you.
2 Corinthians 8:9 — I became poor for you.

Galatians 4:6 — I sent my Son's Spirit into your heart.

Ephesians 2:4 — I am rich in mercy towards you.

Ephesians 3:20 — I give you my power to do more than you can ask.

Colossians 1:13 — I deliver you from the power of darkness.

Colossians 2:13 — I make you alive.

Hebrews 7:25 — I intercede for you.

James 1:18 — I chose to give birth to you.

Revelation 1:5 — I wash you in my own blood.

Workbook: *Understanding Depression*, Turning Point, P. O. Box 22127, Chattanooga, TN 37422-2127

Session  Defenses and Isolation

Session **5**

Personal Preparation: Getting Ready for Session Five

Meet With God

Personal Notes

Do the daily devotion each day (pages 54 to 56) prior to this group meeting.

Self-Awareness

You remember that in our last session we focused on the importance of learning the truth about ourselves from the Bible instead of from our feelings. Instead of defining what our life truly revolves around, faith in Jesus—the light of the world, we are likely to define ourselves around our negative feelings of worthlessness—a black hole.

When we do this, what happens in our lives? How do we relate to others?

Let's talk about isolation and where it usually comes from in our lives. Depression almost always is accompanied by fear and its by-product, anger. There is a fear that our personal failures and inadequacies will be exposed and that shame and humiliation will soon follow. The pressure of this fear leaves a person in a state of perpetual stress. Our thoughts race at night when we are trying to sleep. Angry thoughts fill our minds, and we sometimes fear that we might physically harm someone. Anxiety and dread fill the heart, and every fibre of our being screams out to isolate, to avoid the hurt that will surely come if anyone truly gets to know us. Then a protective pattern sets in and is reinforced because, sure enough, when we do not relate to others, they do not hurt us. Do you recognize the following pattern, leading to the defense of isolation, in your lives?

Fear of shame —> Stress —> Anger —> Anxiety —> Isolation

Is it really effective; that is, does it work to isolate ourselves from others?

What is the downside to isolation?

Most people with depression strongly feel that they must be angry and depressed because of things done to them at an earlier time in life. Might this firm conviction sometimes turn out to be just an inaccurate feeling, a feeling that defends our self-worth from further damage but which locks us in isolation even from our family members?

Leveling

We've been focusing on defenses this session, but before we move on to our Spiritual-Awareness time, I want to change direction for just a minute to talk about something called leveling. To remove one brick at a time from the walls of our defenses, it is important to learn to level.

1. Leveling about our feelings is openly admitting them.

2. To level is to respond openly. Examples: with God (Luke 18:10-14), with self (Romans 12:3), and with others (2 Samuel 12:13).

3. We level when we take the risk of being known by spontaneously reporting our feelings.

Our personal goal should be to replace *isolation* with *sharing*.

What would be the hardest part for you in making that change?

     Workbook: *Understanding Depression*, Turning Point, P. O. Box 22127, Chattanooga, TN 37422-2127

The powerful emotions of fear and anger can cause us problems—particularly when they are hidden behind a wall of defenses and allowed to grow out of control.

I'd encourage you—at some time in the days ahead—to ask God to give you insight into any anger that is bottled up inside, any fears that you're hiding, or any signs of isolation in your life.

The Spiritual-Awareness portion of the meeting focuses on the fourth instruction contained in 2 Peter 1—the addition of courage or self-control to knowledge. The courage or self-control flows from the knowledge of who we are in Christ.

When we are living behind our wall of defenses of anger and isolation, we may feel that we are being courageous and in control, but we actually can be pretty hard to be around. People feel like they have to walk on eggshells around us, and they are likely to stay away from us thus further reinforcing our isolation. The type of courage and self-control that God desires is a fruit of the Spirit and is mentioned in Galatians 5:17 in a list of other traits which helps us see that courage and self-control are other-centered. "But the fruit of the Spirit is love, joy, peace, patience, kindness, goodness, faithfulness, gentleness and self-control" (Galatians 5:22).

In our misguided attempts to get our lives under control, what we actually have done is:

- Push away people who really care about us.
- Allowed our feelings to shape our identity.
- Become slaves to a pattern of isolation.

True courage and self-control do not really take place when
"I" am in control but instead when the Holy Spirit is in control. The Apostle Paul gives a testimony to this problem in his
life. Let's look at Romans 7:14-15. What do you make of his
frequent use of "I" and his spiritual failure?

**Now turn to Romans 8:6. Here Paul tells us the answer to our
failure of self-control. What is it?**

Sometimes we focus on the symptoms and not the cause of
life's problems. If we look at courage and self-control as something we must *work on*, we are likely to soon conclude that *I
can't do it*. Remember in Session Three we saw that the symptoms of depression were debris that rotate in orbit around a
life focus on the **black hole** core of our lives. When life rotates
around God, a different type of *debris* is attracted into rotation
around us. This is just another way of describing the elements
of our pyramid based on 2 Peter 1. Read Romans 8:5-6.

What does our mind-set have to do with having life and peace?

**Read John 15:5. What do Jesus' words have to do with over-
coming depression?**

Sometimes it is hard to *let go and let God* when so much anger
and bitterness invade our lives.

What do you think is God's method for *letting go*?

**Read Colossians 3:13. When we look at forgiving others, are
we called to forgive only those who have asked for forgiveness
and tell us they are sorry?**

A True Story of Forgiving
(Name and some details changed to protect privacy.)

Sarah and her third husband were having problems. She was always angry at him as, in fact, she reported that she had been with her first two husbands. The more she thought about it, the more she recognized she was basically angry at all men. Sarah had been sexually abused by her father from the age of 10 until she left home at 16, having run away with a 20-year-old whom she never married. Sarah was attractive, and prostitution seemed a way not only to support herself but also to manipulate and control men. After nine years of this life, she began to wonder what would happen to her when she was no longer attractive to men. She then went through two marriages, neither of which lasted more than a year. Depression and anger had plagued her life as long as she could remember. One day she decided to attend a neighborhood church in the off chance that she might hear about a God who cared about her. The pastor there took her under his wing and became the first man she had ever trusted.

After a year of attending this church, Sarah married again, this time to a Christian man; but the union lasted for only two years. The pastor could see her anger and irrationality toward her husband and began to ask her more details about the pattern of anger and rejection of men. At this point, she admitted her childhood sexual abuse. She clearly remembered these events, and the issue of supposedly *repressed memories* did not have to be raised. Her pastor told her she needed to go to her father and *level* with him, tell him that his actions toward her had ruined her life but because Christ loved and forgave her, she loved and forgave him. She had been estranged from him for many years and had infrequent contact with him, so this would not happen naturally.

Sarah exploded with indignation and anger. Other friends had counseled her to take her father to court and seek his imprisonment for the rest of his life. That counsel made far more sense to her than that of her pastor. A year went by, and she had not acted on anyone's advice. Then she came to her pastor and told him that the more she read her Bible, the more convinced she had become that he had been right about the need to forgive her father. She asked that he pray for her to have the courage and self-control to do this. About three more months went by before she took the step. The results were transforming both for her and her father. A new courage entered her life to trust God the Father (a masculine title!), and she began a rapid spiritual growth. Her depression was almost entirely gone, and indeed she found that she had been given by God everything she needed to be happy and productive. Her father began attending church with her and soon received Christ as his Savior. He confessed his guilt and shame to his daughter and to the Lord and was truly set free. For the first time ever, they began to enjoy a true and godly father/daughter relationship.

Sarah never looked again into her past, her shame and guilt. Neither did she ever again burn with anger and resentment against her father.

As we discussed a few weeks ago, spiritual depression is always a part of the mix, including the biological and psychological. D. Martyn Lloyd-Jones writes in his magnificent book, *Spiritual Depression*:

> Would you like to be rid of this spiritual depression? . . . I say, therefore, that this is the test, that you acknowledge readily and say clearly that you look to Christ and to Christ alone and to nothing and no one else, that you stop looking at particular sins and particular people. Look at nothing and nobody but look entirely to Christ and say:
> "My hope is built on nothing less
> Than Jesus' blood and righteousness
> I dare not trust the sweetest frame,
> But wholly lean on Jesus' name.
> On Christ the Solid Rock I stand,
> All other ground is sinking sand."

This story is based on the author's experience while working with Understanding Depression *groups. The names have been changed to protect the privacy of the individual.*

Workbook: *Understanding Depression*, Turning Point, P. O. Box 22127, Chattanooga, TN 37422-2127

So far we have talked about Bible truth in regard to living a new life, but we have not specifically tried to apply it to ourselves. Prayer is sometimes a way of appropriating the promises of God for our lives. I'd like to invite you to pray for some of the things we've talked about, such as:

- Our powerlessness to have courage and self-control on our own.

- The influence of what we set our minds on.

- The role of forgiveness in being able to set our minds on God and to forget about the past.

In view of these things, are there other areas you need to remember in prayer? Describe.

➜ **Day One**

Scripture: Read 1 Corinthians 2:12-16 and Romans 8:15.

Questions for Meditation:

1. According to Romans 8:15, what is one key thing that the Spirit who is from God allows us to understand that He has freely given us?

2. Instead of irritability in our relationships with others, what does 1 Corinthians 1:13 tell us we can expect, by the Spirit's power, to be in our speech now?

3. If it is true that "the man without the Spirit does not accept the things that come from the Spirit of God, for they are foolishness to him, and he cannot understand them, because they are spiritually discerned" (1 Corinthians 2:14), how can you continue to live and walk by the Spirit?

4. What does it mean in your life when Paul says, "But we have the mind of Christ" (1 Corinthians 2:16) ?

Suggestions for Prayer:

1. Try listening to Christian music while you pray or sing your own hymns or spiritual songs so that you might make this prayer time a time of worship.

2. Thank God for giving you the Spirit and the mind of Christ. Be bold and let your faith reach out to receive these promises of things already given to you.

3. Look back at one of last week's daily devotional Scripture statements about who you are in Christ and what it means to have His mind. Then thank God for each of them, consciously claiming each promise as your own.

➜ **Day Two**

Scripture: Read Ephesians 5:18-20.

Questions for Meditation:

1. If the infilling of the Holy Spirit leads to an experience of "getting high" such as Paul suggests, have you experienced this?

2. Since Paul says, "Speak to one another with psalms, hymns and spiritual songs. Sing and make music in your heart to

the Lord" (verse 19), are you finding it easier to get into meaningful "one another" relationships, especially in spiritual settings with music? Why or why not?

3. Paul also advises "always giving thanks to God the Father for everything, in the name of our Lord Jesus Christ" (verse 20). Can you even thank God for your depression and how you are growing spiritually because of it?

Suggestions for Prayer:

1. Pray thanksgiving for all the trials and hardships of your life, one by one.

2. Thank God for the meaningful future that is yours by faith, not by feelings.

→ **Day Three**

Scripture: Read John 15:1-4.

Questions for Meditation:

1. What "branches" has the Father cut off in your life, and what others will He probably also desire to cut off?

2. What is a fruit-bearing branch?

3. What branches are in your life that may need further pruning even though they even now bear some fruit?

4. In verse 3, what is the assurance that this pruning is not a rejection of you?

5. What could you do to remain even closer to the "vine"?

Suggestions for Prayer:

1. Thank God for the pruning He has done.

2. Invite Him to prune even more.

3. Ask Him to empower you by His Spirit to abide more closely with Jesus.

→ **Day Four**

Scripture: Read Galatians 5:14-18.

Questions for Meditation:

1. Since the law commands us to love "our neighbor"; that is, everyone, as ourselves, are we able to do so by willing it to be so?

2. What is the consequence for us if we allow irritability to rule our lives?

3. If the answer is to "live by the Spirit," do I really know what that means?

4. Paul says if you walk in the Spirit, "You are not under law" (verse 18). Why is it important not to be under the law even if it is God's own good and perfect law? For help, see Romans 5:20.

Suggestions for Prayer:

1. Pray for the people who irritate you the most and ask God to bless them. (It's hard to stay angry at people for whom you pray!)

2. As in yesterday's devotion, pray for a closer relationship with Jesus, "the vine."

3. Pray that the deeds of your sinful nature may be crucified with Christ, not only in fact but also in experience.

➜ Day Five

Scripture: Read Romans 8:1-2.

Questions for Meditation:

1. Are you "in Christ Jesus"?

2. Do you believe that God holds no condemnation toward you?

3. According to verse 2, is this because of you?

4. What is the "law of the Spirit of life"? (You may want to read all of Chapter 8 to grasp the sense of this.)

Suggestions for Prayer:

1. Thank God for the free gift of faith that makes you "in Christ Jesus."

2. Thank God that although you deserve to be condemned by Him, you are not because the blood of Jesus has washed you clean.

3. Thank God that when God looks at you, He sees Jesus.

4. Pray fervently for the Spirit-filled life so that you might live in courage and Christ-control.

 Workbook: *Understanding Depression*, Turning Point, P. O. Box 22127, Chattanooga, TN 37422-2127

Meet With God

Personal Notes

Do the daily devotion each day (pages 65 to 69) prior to this group meeting.

Self-Awareness

Many people with depression find themselves almost preoccupied with a thought pattern that goes something like this:

> You are really a failure at everything you have tried to do. If you tried to make friends, you'd never succeed. No one wants a loser like you for a friend. People avoid you like the plague, and even your own family can't stand you. Come to think of it, the world would really be a better place if you weren't in it. Why don't you just go ahead and end it all now?

Have you had to contend with thoughts like this?

When we listen to this sort of accusation, we begin to feel it is true. We have already talked about our need to look at ourselves in the light of the truth of the Bible, not our feelings. When these thoughts of negative accusation against ourselves come to mind, it appears to us that it is just simply our own minds affirming the truth about our failures and the accusations seem so real that we have trouble reminding ourselves that they contradict the truth of the Bible.

What do you do about it when these heavy accusations are dumped on your head?

Before we move on to our time of Spiritual-Awareness, I'd like to talk with you about something called *carefronting*. In his book *Caring Enough to Confront*, David Augsburger originates the term *carefronting*. Augsburger introduces us to this idea of carefronting as a communication technique that brings together the positive idea of **caring** with the negative idea of **confronting**.

Now we are ready to get a little more direct in helping each other to see the ways in which we have allowed satanic attacks to influence our lives. See pages 59 & 60.

Workbook: *Understanding Depression*, Turning Point, P. O. Box 22127, Chattanooga, TN 37422-2127

Communication by Loving Confrontation

Caring + Confronting = Carefronting

Carefronting is confronting in a caring way. The caring must be genuine, and the confronting must be motivated by love, not anger. Carefronting is a way to communicate the truth in a loving way—with both impact and respect.

Carefronting says, "I care enough to confront. I want a relationship, and I also want honesty and integrity." In the process of carefronting, conflict is viewed as *neutral* (neither good nor bad) and *natural* (neither to be avoided nor short-circuited).

Carefronting brings together these elements of caring and confronting:

Caring	and	Confronting
I want a relationship with you	and	I want honesty and integrity.
I care about our relationship	and	I feel deeply about this issue.
I want to hear your view	and	I want to express my view clearly.
I want to respect your insights	and	I want respect for mine.
I give you my loving, honest respect	and	I want you to know where I stand and what I am feeling, needing, and wanting a response.

Carefronting invites another to change but does not demand it. By communicating the truth in love, we create an environment for healing and growth. Carefronting and the convicting work of the Holy Spirit go hand in hand in freeing a person from a life-controlling problem.

Ways of Carefronting Without Being Judgmental

Focus your feedback on the action, not on the actor.
This gives the person the freedom to change their behavior without feeling personal rejection. Example: "When someone criticizes people who are not present, as you were doing a moment ago, I get uptight. I'd encourage you to say what you have to say to the person."

Focus your feedback on your observations, not on your conclusions.
Comment on what you have actually seen or heard, not on what you think, imagine, or infer. When you state your own opinions and conclusions, your words will evoke immediate defensiveness. Focus instead on a statement of fact. Example: "You are not looking at me and not answering when I speak. Please give me your attention and an answer."

Focus your feedback on descriptions, not on judgments.
Do not comment on another's behavior as nice or rude, right or wrong. Use a clear, accurate description in neutral language. Be a reporter and not a judge. Example: "I see that you avoid looking at me when I speak and seem anxious for our sessions to end. Why is that?"

Focus feedback on ideas, information, and alternatives—not on advice and answers.
Instead of commenting with instructions on what to do with the data you have to offer, offer ideas, options, and alternatives. Example: "It appears that you face several options."

Focus feedback not on why, but on what and how.
Don't judge a person's values, motives, and intents. Instead, focus on observable actions, words, or tone of voice. You can best help a person to see himself or herself by focusing on what, where, when, and how.

When you are carefronting, it should be done carefully, lovingly, gently, constructively, and clearly. Never carefront with any possible interpretations of blaming, shaming, or punishing.

Used by permission. Taken from *Caring Enough to Confront* by David Augsburger, copyright by Herald Press, 1980, Scottdale, PA 15683.

Today we will add another dimension to our struggle with feelings of worthlessness. It is the world of demonic spiritual opposition. This is not to say that depression is a form of demon possession though rarely it may be. In his first letter, Peter writes: "Be self-controlled and alert. Your enemy the devil prowls around like a roaring lion looking for someone to devour" (1 Peter 5:8). Peter wrote this to all Christians, not just those with depression; however, depression opens a window of opportunity for a particular type of attack.

A lion on the hunt seeks to separate the vulnerable from the pack. Smaller, less confident animals, those on the fringe of the herd become their chosen prey. Christians are always attacked in the most vulnerable and least-confident part of their make-up too. Depression creates a window of vulnerability in the area of self-worth.

Who is this devil, and what are demons? The Bible tells us that sometime long ago in God's creation, there was a powerful and beautiful archangel who led a rebellion of some of the angels in heaven against God. He and these angels were defeated by the archangel Michael and the remaining loyal and faithful angels, and they were cast out of heaven and down upon the earth. These fallen angels are known in the Bible as demons, and the beautiful angel as the devil or Satan. It is about their activities in the world today that our Spiritual Awareness time will focus.

Spiritual-Awareness

In order to fight against the spiritual forces of the devil, our Spiritual-Awareness emphasis is on the addition of yet another quality of the Christian life from our theme passage of 2 Peter 1—fortitude—or in the NIV Bible, perseverance. Our passage defines these big words as "a dogged determination to keep going." More commonly, it is known as "hang in there, baby!"

As we add to our pyramid one more ingredient, we remind ourselves again that these qualities are already ours in Christ Jesus. Peter simply urges us to take hold and put on these things that have been given us for happiness and productivity of life.

The Greek word for fortitude has the underlying meaning of hopefulness; that is, as we stand in the battle of life, we do so with hopeful anticipation for we know that "if God is for us, who can be against us?" (Romans 8:31). This includes the devil.

Read Romans 5:3-4. Here the word fortitude is translated as perseverance. What does this tell us about the suffering that is a part of depression? Does it encourage us to believe that what we have been through will lead to a new sense of hope?

Let's be clear that we are called to persistence in following God as the One who delivers us, not persistence in accepting depression. It means there may not be an instant deliverance in God but that we must persist in waging the war against the world, our own sinful nature, and the devil—a war which will be won in Christ Jesus.

Today we want to emphasize the war against the devil. It is a very real war. We talked earlier about the constant accusation of worthlessness which we feel. Turn to Revelation 12:10-11 so that we can see the true source of these thoughts.

When we go out the door in the day and feel accused of inadequacy and when we toss and turn on our beds in the middle of the night filled with a sense of shame and despair, who is really accusing us?

The original temptation of Adam and Eve in the Garden of Eden involved a bit of truth about eating the forbidden fruit followed by a big distortion of the words God had spoken to Adam (Genesis 3:1-5).

Have you ever noticed that the "tape" which the devil plays in your mind contains a kernel of truth but then draws conclusions which contradict God's Word?

Turn in your Bible to John 8:44. Here Jesus is speaking to the Pharisees, a group of legalistic Jews. What does He say about the devil?

There is another motive in the devil's mind when he attacks us. Let's read John 10:10. Who is "the thief"?

In the passage from Revelation 12, what two things did the saints of old use to overcome this accusing voice?

If the martyred saints of old overcame the terrible accusations of the devil by their testimony, so too must we proceed. Martin Luther, the founder of the Reformation of the Church in the 16th century, struggled against depression all of his life. Nevertheless, he lived victoriously, and his life changed the whole course of Western history. In his daily times of prayer, his confession of faith was open and verbal, and he often shouted at the devil such things as, "Devil, I defy your accusations in the name of Jesus. You are a liar who will suffer forever in the lake of fire. In the name of Jesus, I command you out of my mind!" Another great Christian who also fought a life-long battle with depression was the English preacher and author Charles Spurgeon. He too knew how to use the Word of God against the devil. Although Spurgeon has been dead for nearly 100 years, his books as well as Luther's are still in print and touching new generations of believers. Your life can be effective also, and the world can be a better place because you lived.

Turn now to Matthew 4:1-11. If even Jesus had to be tempted by the devil, won't you and I also be tempted? How did Jesus show fortitude and perseverance in His spiritual battle? In the course of these 40 days, what did He use to combat the devil? What was the outcome of it all?

Hollywood has made the devil and demonic activity seem mysterious and frightening. Let's see what God says to a Christian about this. Turn to 1 John 4:2-4 and consider the following three questions:

- **How do you know if you have the Spirit of God?**

- **Who is the antichrist?**

- **How do you know you can overcome the power of the antichrist?**

Sometimes it is helpful or even necessary to have another believer stand with you in prayer at times of the greatest spiritual attack.

Remember, our key ingredient this week is fortitude or perseverance. Spiritual warfare is a lifetime challenge for all Christians.

Do you have such a person you could turn to?

Today, make this time of application of these biblical truths also a time of prayer. Much of spiritual warfare is waged in prayer. If there are any particular spiritual attacks you would like us to pray against, please feel free to write them down. Bring your request to the next session. We read in Hebrews 12:1, "Therefore, since we are surrounded by such a great cloud of witnesses, let us throw off everything that hinders and the sin that so easily entangles, and let us run with perseverance the race marked out for us." Here again we find our theme word "perseverance," and it is a part of our effort to throw off the "sin that so easily entangles." So, let's agree to pray and show fortitude and perseverance in fighting the great spiritual battle against depression.

Write a prayer concerning your spiritual battle against depression.

   Workbook: *Understanding Depression*, Turning Point, P. O. Box 22127, Chattanooga, TN 37422-2127

↦ **Day One**

Scripture: Read Jude verse 6.

Questions for Meditation:

1. Who are "the angels who did not keep their positions of authority but abandoned their own home"?

2. If they are "kept in darkness, bound with everlasting chains," how can it be that they are free to attack you?

3. Martin Luther once compared the demonic forces to a dog on a chain. It was restrained, but if anyone tempted it by going within the distance of its chain, the person would be bitten. How might this cast some light on the previous question?

4. What sort of thoughts or actions might you be doing that puts you within the length of the devil's chain?

Suggestions for Prayer:

1. Thank God for the great truth John writes about in 1 John 4:4: "You, dear children, are from God and have overcome them, because the one who is in you is greater than the one who is in the world." Pray that when the devil and his demonic forces attack you, you will be bold to resist them.

2. Thank God you are a temple of the Holy Spirit who lives in you (1 Corinthians 6:19) and that the Spirit's power has already overcome Satan. Thank Him that wherever you are, this spiritual power and armor go with you.

3. Confess any ways you have been allowing room in your life for demonic oppression or temptation and ask for cleansing and forgiveness in the blood of Jesus.

4. Pray aloud in the name of Jesus against the demonic powers that have accused you this week. Name these accusations as best you can; for example, despair, guilt, shame, etc.

↦ **Day Two**

Scripture: Read Ephesians 6:10-18.

Questions for Meditation:

1. This picture of spiritual armor is taken from a description of the battle armor of a Roman soldier. Did you notice there is no armor on the backside? Why do you think this is? Are you willing to face Satan head on?

2. In verse 10, whose power are we looking for?

3. In verse 11, the words, "the devil's schemes," can also be translated "the devil's expert methods." Are you up against an amateur? Do you not have to be careful lest you fall for the devil's expert accusations against you?

4. Are the devil's accusations against you true according to the Bible?

5. Verse 12 says "our struggle is not against flesh and blood, but against the rulers, against the authorities, against the powers of this dark world and against the spiritual forces of evil in the heavenly realms." Have you thought about the times when you are so angry with people that perhaps it is not really they but instead demonic forces that are battling against you?

6. Verse 13 speaks of "the day of evil." Apparently some days are more likely to contain demonic attack than others, but the need is to be prepared every day. Are you now in "a day of assault from the evil one"?

7. Verses 14 and 15 tell us to put on three pieces of armor: truth, righteousness, and the gospel of peace. Based on the Bible, what do you think these three things are? Why do they cover these particular parts of the body?

8. In addition, in verse 16 Paul says that faith is something like a shield which must be taken up in order to fend off the devil's flaming arrows. Have you thought about faith as something to be exercised? If so, how do you do it?

9. In verse 17, we need to cover our heads (our minds?) with the helmet of salvation. What does this mean?

10. Verse 17 also tells us to take up the sword of the Spirit and tells us that it is the Bible. Do you travel constantly with your sword sharp and ready?

11. Verse 18 tells us that in addition to the sword, prayer is an offensive weapon of our spiritual warfare. Why do you suppose it jumps from a list of things we do for ourselves to a call to "always keep on praying for all the saints"?

Workbook: *Understanding Depression*, Turning Point, P. O. Box 22127, Chattanooga, TN 37422-2127

Suggestions for Prayer:

1. Pray verse by verse for yourself using the answers to the above questions as your guide.

2. Pray for "all the saints," especially for those in the depression group.

→ **Day Three**

Scripture: Read James 4:7-8.

Questions for Meditation:

1. Why does submitting oneself to God come before resisting the devil?

2. Do you suppose the devil does not flee from us and our shouted rebukes of him because we are not truly submitted to God?

3. Read Romans 12:1. Does this help you to understand submission to God? Have you done it?

4. Verse 8 calls us to come near to God, another way of expressing the thought in Romans 12:1. Has God come near to you? How can you tell?

5. From the last part of verse 8, we see that double-mindedness inhibits truly coming near to God. Are you double-minded about some things you know God is calling you to?

Suggestions for Prayer:

1. With Romans 12:1 open in front of you, prayerfully give your body to the Lord. Remember, when you give Him your body, it includes everything in it: heart, soul, mind, and spirit.

2. In prayer, deliberately come close to God. Because the Spirit lives in you, you are free to sit in his lap and call him "Daddy" (see Romans 8:15) knowing that unlike human fathers, He is absolutely loving and kind, seeking only good things for you.

3. Pray against the "spirit of slavery to fear" (Romans 8:15) using the name of Jesus against this demonic spirit. Identify in your pray every fear you can think of.

4. Confess to God the things you thought of that involve double-mindedness on your part and ask His forgiveness.
Then praise and thank Him for loving and forgiving you.

→ **Day Four**

Scripture: Read James 5:11 and Job 1:6-12.

Questions for Meditation:

1. Again in James 5:11, we see the association of our theme
word, fortitude or perseverance, with spiritual warfare. The
book of Job is the story of everyone with depression, and
its basic message is the essential requirement to "keep on
keeping on" in the face of seemingly never-ending oppression and crushing circumstance. How do you think it was
possible for Job to say after months and perhaps even years
of loss and sickness, "Though he slay me, yet will I hope in
him" (Job 13:15)?

2. Was Satan free to attack Job without the Lord's permission?

3. Job was a man of faith, a man whose "goodness" was established not because he was by nature such a good man but
because by faith he had been declared blameless and he
lived by faith daily. Why would God give Satan permission
to attack him so strongly? (In considering your answer, you
might remember the last part of our theme passage, 2 Peter 1:

> **Nevertheless,**
> **we need occasional reminders and challenges,**
> **for, it seems, we are quick to slack off**
> **when life becomes comfortable or the road ahead**
> **appears a little easier to negotiate.**
> **This may well be one of the reasons our loving God**
> **permits suffering to afflict us;**
> **it keeps our heads straight and our hearts focused**
> **on the truly important goal of our lives,**
> **a right relationship with God.**

4. Though faith must be tested in order to remain strong, it is
God's ordinary plan to put a hedge of protection around
His children. Is the hedge up or down in your life right
now? Why do you think yes or no?

5. Do you think the Lord may allow Satan to test you in an
area of your life? (Read 2 Corinthians 12:7 in preparation
for your answer.)

Workbook: *Understanding Depression*, Turning Point, P. O. Box 22127, Chattanooga, TN 37422-2127

6. Did Paul's "thorn" (2 Corinthians 12:7) make him a depressed and ineffective person? Can you trust God that any thorn He may leave in your life will not make you a depressed and ineffective person either?

Suggestions for Prayer:

1. Thank God for the things that have been accomplished in your character because of your depression.

2. Thank God that you are "convinced that neither death nor life, neither angels nor demons, neither the present nor the future, nor any powers, neither height nor depth, nor anything else in all creation, will be able to separate us from the love of God that is in Christ Jesus our Lord" (Romans 8:38-39).

3. People who have had depression are typically extremely effective ministers to others who hurt and suffer, and the church would be sorely lacking without them. Ask God to teach you anything you need to learn from your experience with depression.

4. Pray a hedge of protection around yourself and your family.

→ **Day Five**

Today we will look at several Bible passages that deal with our spiritual warfare. Look at each of them, meditate upon them, and pray whatever thoughts the Spirit puts on your heart.

Matthew 6:13
Matthew 25:41
Luke 8:15
Luke 10:17-19
Luke 13:16
Luke 21:19
John 8:44
John 17:15
Acts 10:37-38
Romans 8:25
Romans 15:4
Romans 16:20
2 Corinthians 11:14
Ephesians 4:26-27
James 1:2-4
Revelation 3:10

Session **7** *Changing Old Ways of Coping*

eet With God

Personal Notes

Do the daily devotion each day (pages 75 to 78) prior to this group meeting.

elf-Awareness

Over the past six weeks, we've talked together in our group about many things involved in our struggle with depression, and we've learned from each other's experiences. Our Self-Awareness sessions each week have dealt with the key areas of winning the battle. Now we are going to shift gears and focus more on applying all of these things to our lives by ministering to one another.

As we prepare for this session, I would like to remind you of three things God has given us in our fight against depression, things we have talked about in earlier sessions: (1) the Word of God as described in Hebrews 4:12, "For the word of God is living and active. Sharper than any double-edged sword, it penetrates even to dividing soul and spirit, joints and marrow; it judges the thoughts and attitudes of the heart," (2) the Spirit of God as described in John 16:13, "But when he, the Spirit of truth, comes, he will guide you into all truth. He will not speak on his own; he will speak only what he hears, and he will tell you what is yet to come," and (3) the people of God as described in Hebrews 3:13, "But encourage one another daily, as long as it is called Today, so that none of you may be hardened by sin's deceitfulness."

The first two things we have talked a great deal about in our previous sessions, but the last, the "one another" relationships of the Christian life, we have avoided. In our next session we are going to begin an exercise that is based on that model, and it will encourage the kind of interaction that those "one

 Workbook: *Understanding Depression*, Turning Point, P. O. Box 22127, Chattanooga, TN 37422-2127

another" verses describe. We will invite several volunteers from our group to give a brief history of their depression or an awareness they have gained about depression and share how God is working to help them overcome their despair. Then the other group members will be asked to give constructive feedback about what they have heard.

How do you feel about letting another caring person help you see yourself clearly?

How do you feel about ministering to others in the group by being a caring listener?

All through the Bible, we find "one another" Scriptures that instruct us in the kinds of caring actions and attitudes that ought to characterize our relationships as brothers and sisters in Christ. Let's look at a few of those "one another" verses.

1 Peter 1:22 says, "Love one another deeply, from the heart."

Galatians 5:13 tells us to "serve one another in love."

Galatians 6:2 points to a need: "Carry each other's burdens."

Ephesians 4:32 suggests an attitude: "Be kind and compassionate to one another."

Now, we will build another level on our pyramid which we have called surrender to God's purposes or godliness in the NIV Bible translation. One of God's purposes for His people is that they live in mutual love and support in one-another relationships.

What are some ways in which a trusted, caring, Christian friend can help us walk with God?

As we have been building our pyramid week by week, it is sure- ly no accident that the Holy Spirit working through Peter chose the sequence of steps that He did. A literal translation of 2 Peter 1 tells us to add each step to the previous one. In a sense, therefore, each step becomes a foundation and leads to the next one. These steps are already given to us by God. We do these things only by appropriating the things we have. You may already have a million dollars in the bank, but if you nev- er go and make a withdrawal, it will do you no good. We need the encouragement of one-another relationships with other believers in order to make these withdrawals from the deposit God has made to our accounts.

By way of review, we see that the gift of faith is the foundation of the whole pyramid. Faith is the hand that reaches out to re- ceive each of the following steps, each of which in turn nudges us upward to the next one. First, faith takes hold of the nature of God, and goodness begins to form in our char- acter. As our lives shift toward this more healthy way of living, faith again reaches out to add a hunger for truth to our make- up, and we are no longer content to live by the wisdom of this world. Then as the truth contained in God's Word pours into us, we begin to develop courage to go on and trust God for a new life. We quickly find ourselves in a spiritual battle with the forces of darkness which seek to keep us from a new and ef- fective life, but courageous faith reaches out to add fortitude or perseverance so that we don't give up. By our persistent "stick-to-it-iveness," faith then leads us to see that we won't tru- ly become the godly person we want to be without surrender to His purposes—which is where we are this week. Remember, the devil will try to criticize and tear you down by telling you that you don't have these qualities, but he is a liar!

If adding or appropriating these things by faith is God's call on our lives, then how do we develop our next level? Actually, the literal translation of this level is *godliness*. Our theme pas- sage from 2 Peter 1 in its paraphrase version describes the method of appropriating godliness: Surrender to God's pur- poses. Peter correctly believes that if we do the faith act, godli- ness will of necessity appear.

In an earlier session, we looked at Romans 12:1. Let's look at it again, and this time add verse 2.

What two things does Paul call on us to do?

If we do this, what does Paul say will be the result?

Workbook: *Understanding Depression*, Turning Point, P. O. Box 22127, Chattanooga, TN 37422-2127

Is this result perhaps a definition of godliness?

A literal translation of the first part of Romans 12:2 is "keep on not conforming to the patterns of this world." Here is the idea again of last week's session, persistent fortitude and endurance.

Have you ever had the experience of rejecting the world's ways one day and the next having taken them back again? What do you then do? Just give up?

If godliness is something to be put on by surrender, the Bible should tell us more about this. In fact, the Apostle Paul does use language like this in several places. Let's look at Colossians 3:4-10. When the Bible talks about *putting off* and *putting on*, this is appropriation language; that is, these are things we already have by faith in Christ. We therefore need only to **take hold** of them, not **do** them. In verse 9, it says we have already taken off our old selves.

When did we do that?

In verse 10, it says we have already put on the new self.

When did we do that?

Let's look at one more passage that speaks to appropriating or taking hold of the new life of godliness. What does 1 Timothy 6:11-12 say about this?

Active faith is, in a sense, contagious. That is, when we are around people who are "taking hold" of the promises of God, we also become bold to do so. Let's look at two verses that show us how essential it is that we look to one another as we seek to overcome depression: 1 Corinthians 12:26-27 and Galatians 6:2. Let's discuss three questions that arise from these verses.

Why does Paul say it matters to each of us what other Christians are going through?

What are some ways in which we might carry each other's burdens?

What is the "law of Christ"?

Let's look at one more verse. "Therefore encourage one another and build each other up, just as in fact you are doing" (1 Thessalonians 5:11). Paul takes the words right out of my mouth. This is what this *Understanding Depression* group is all about.

pplication

The application of godliness or surrender to God's purposes will require some spiritual discipline as we seek to appropriate these promises of God's Word daily. Some of them we can do alone, and they will be included in this week's daily devotions. However, one of them will require a regular "one-another" relationship.

How do you feel about developing a regular "one-another relationship"?

Write a prayer about a regular one-another relationship.

Workbook: *Understanding Depression*, Turning Point, P. O. Box 22127, Chattanooga, TN 37422-2127

→ **Day One**

Today and tomorrow, we will use our devotion time to look at
two of the most important spiritual disciplines: Bible reading
and prayer. Today we will look at Bible reading.

Scripture: Read Matthew 4:4 and Psalm 119:89-105.

Questions for Meditation:

1. According to Jesus, what is more important than food?

2. To whom did Jesus say these words?

3. Do you suppose you too could defeat the devil with God's
   Word from the Bible?

4. According to Psalm 119:89, does God's Word ever change?

5. According to the psalmist (verses 92-93), what would have
   happened to him if he had not delighted in reading God's
   Word? ("Law" here means all of Scripture.)

6. According to verse 95, what rescues us from wicked people?

7. According to verse 96, what is even better than perfection?

8. What makes you wiser than your enemies (verse 98)?

9. What two mighty qualities does one obtain from God's
   Word (verses 99-100)?

10. Does God's Word make life taste sweet(verse 103)?

11. According to verses 104-105, what does reading God's
    Word have to do with guidance?

12. Do you have a plan for regular, personal Bible reading?

Suggestion for Prayer:

> Pray for yourself that God's Word would work in you the
> same thing that Paul prayed for the Christians in the
> church at Ephesus (Ephesians 2:14-21).

→ **Day Two**

Prayer is one of the most essential spiritual disciplines. Look up each of the following verses and then pray about them:

James 5:16—Pray for each other. It makes a difference!
Matthew 5:44—Pray for your enemies.
Mark 11:24—Faith is exercised in prayer.
Luke 18:1—Never give up on prayer!
Romans 8:26—The Spirit joins our prayers.
Ephesians 6:18—Pray persistently in the Spirit for all the saints.
Philippians 4:6—Prayer—an antidote to anxiety!
Colossians 4:2—Be devoted, watchful, and thankful in prayer.
1 Thessalonians 5:17—Pray continually.
1 Timothy 2:8—Pray without anger or quarreling.
1 Timothy 4:4-5—Prayer makes things good.
James 5:13—Prayer—the only thing to do in times of trouble.
I John 5:16—Pray for others in sin.

→ **Day Three**

Scripture: Read Romans 12:4-21.

Questions for Meditation:

1. What do you think your spiritual gift might be, and how could it be used in the group next week?

2. Have you ever considered what it means that "each member belongs to all the others"?

3. Could you apply some of things in verses 11-13 to your prayer partner/mutual mentor?

4. What things do you see listed in verses 14-21 that you need to exercise your faith and take hold of?

5. Are you "faithful in prayer"?

Suggestions for Prayer:

1. If you do not know what your spiritual gifts are, pray that God will lead you to a knowledge and understanding of them.

2. Pray for a desire in your heart to trust other believers, especially your prayer partner.

3. Pray for your prayer partner.

   Workbook: *Understanding Depression*, Turning Point, P. O. Box 22127, Chattanooga, TN 37422-2127

4. Pray for those who persecute you.

5. Pray prayers of appropriation for those things that you see from these verses which are not functioning in your life right now.

↝ Day Four

Scripture: Read Romans 15:1-7.

Questions for Meditation:

1. As you think about your prayer partner in light of verse 1, which of you do you think might be weaker? What does this mean for your next conversation?

2. Are you building up your neighbor? Your prayer partner?

3. Since Paul means the Old Testament by "everything that was written in the past" (verse 4), are you reading there with some regularity?

4. Why does verse 4 say it is necessary to do this?

5. As God gives you "endurance and encouragement" through the Bible, what else will He give you in regard to your fellow believers?

6. If you are to "accept one another that then, just as Christ accepted you" (verse 7), what will this mean that needs to change in your life?

Suggestions for Prayer:

1. Pray for your prayer partner; pray about your ministry to this person.

2. Pray for a desire to read the Old Testament.

3. Pray that the Holy Spirit will enlighten the eyes of your heart to understand Scripture.

4. Pray for the things you identified in response to question 6 above.

↝ Day Five

Scripture: Read Colossians 3:1-17.

Questions for Meditation:

1. Here we have even more "appropriation" language; that is, God's call to put on what He has already given to us. Have you set your heart and mind on things above? If you have not as much as you would wish, does Romans 12:1-2 help?

2. Paul says the reason you can do this is that you "died." In what way and when did you die? (If you need help, see Romans 6:1-11.)

3. What is the glorious future that awaits you? (Colossians 3: 4)

4. Is there anything on the "put to death" list that applies to you?

5. Paul says you "used to" do these things, but then he goes on as if you still do. How can it be both ways at the same time? What does "appropriation" have to do with truly getting "used to" into the past?

6. Have you put on the new self as defined in Romans 12:1? Are these not fruit of the Spirit that produce themselves as you daily "offer your bodies as living sacrifices" to God?

7. Read again Colossians 3:13. Have you done this with everyone?

8. What again does Paul mean by "put on" (Colossians 3:14)? How do you do it?

9. In Colossians 3:16, "admonish" one another means not only to correct but also to remind and caution. Are you willing to do this with your prayer partner?

10. Colossians 3:17 tells you the source of your victory in all of these things. Are you now ready to use the name of the One through whom you may now turn to the Father in prayer?

Suggestions for Prayer:

1. Pray about your answers to each of above 10 questions.

2. Pray for your prayer partner.

   Workbook: *Understanding Depression*, Turning Point, P. O. Box 22127, Chattanooga, TN 37422-2127

Session **8** *Ministering to One Another*

Meet With God

Personal Notes

Do the daily devotion each day (pages 83 to 87) prior to this group meeting.

Self-Awareness

It has been suggested that many times a perfect stranger can learn more about us in half an hour than we discover in years of self-examination. That may or may not be true, but there's no question that we do need caring Christian friends who will be lovingly honest with us. This is God's plan for His family. He has given us three important resources to help us in our walk of faith: the Word of God, the Spirit of God, and the *people of God*. We are to have a ministry to *one another* in the body of Christ.

Read the verses listed here. What does each say about what should characterize our ministry to each other?

Romans 15:7

1 John 4:7, 11

1 Corinthians 12:25

After our first session of ministry to one another, think about what was useful and valuable in that experience. Write down your thoughts.

What is the value to the person who is sharing from his or her life?

What is the value to the listener?

Spiritual Awareness:

In 2 Peter 1:7 we read, "And to [your] godliness, [add] brotherly kindness."

It's not hard to imagine how a person who has developed the quality of godliness would begin to reflect God's attitude outwardly—to the people around them.

Brotherly kindness here specifically relates to kindness exercised *within the family of God*. It involves caring for our brothers (and our sisters) in Christ. It is affection that grows out of common interests and concern—and those commonalities draw us together.

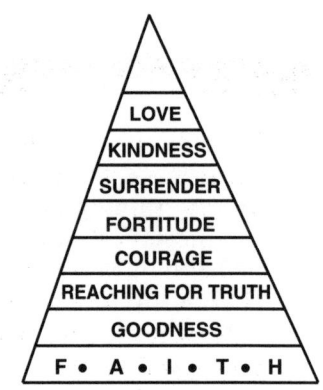

In what ways do you think brotherly kindness would show itself? What kinds of attitudes and actions would result from brotherly kindness?

What did you witness in our peer ministry time that is an example of brotherly kindness?

Let's see what else God's Word has to say about the subject of kindness and compassion toward our brothers and sisters in the faith.

Workbook: *Understanding Depression*, Turning Point, P. O. Box 22127, Chattanooga, TN 37422-2127

Romans 12:10
What does this say about the degree of our love for other Christians?

How would you put that verse into action?

Luke 10:33-35
The Samaritan in Jesus' story is an example of brotherly kindness. Jesus used this story to explain what He meant when He said, "Love your neighbor as yourself" (verse 27).

We can learn from the example of the Samaritan about how to show brotherly kindness and compassion for others.

What are some of the things the Samaritan did for this man in trouble? What is the *first* thing he did?

Then what action did he take?

What does this example say to you about the people around you who are in trouble?

1 Peter 1:22
How does this verse describe the love that we demonstrate within the body of Christ?

Hebrews 10:24-25
How can we spur one another on toward love and good deeds?

What two instructions do we find in verse 25? Why are they important?

What indicates that some people may have been withdrawing or isolating themselves?

John 13:34-35
These words are found among Christ's final instructions to His disciples, and that gives them some added emphasis.

How do we know that Jesus isn't just making a casual suggestion here?

How are we to love one another?

He is the example for the kind of love for one another that should characterize our lives.

What is so unique about the love of Christians that Jesus could say "all men will know that you are my disciples, if you love one another" (verse 35)?

What kinds of things do we do in showing Christian love and brotherly kindness that grab the attention of those outside of the faith?

 **pplication**

There is a bumper sticker out that picks up the thought behind the Galatians 6:10 passage we just looked at: "Do Acts of Random Kindness!" Or as Paul put it, "As we have opportunity, let us do good to all people, especially to those who belong to the family of believers." You have all been doing acts of kindness for each other all last week during your daily contacts.

What might you like to have done differently now that you have served each other this way?

How do you feel about the opportunity to minister kindness for another week to your prayer partner?

Workbook: *Understanding Depression*, Turning Point, P. O. Box 22127, Chattanooga, TN 37422-2127

→ **Day One**

Scripture: Read Acts 14:8-17.

Questions for Meditation:

1. The greatest example of kindness is that shown by God toward us, His children. As this lesson shows, even when we do acts of kindness for others and if they are truly biblical kindnesses, they are the acts of God at work in us. Do you believe that God might show you His kindness by completely healing you of your depression? Why or why not?

2. In verse 9, what was one ingredient in the crippled man's healing?

3. There are biblical examples of people of faith not receiving healing. Why do you think this might be? Could the sovereignty of God's will be a mystery to human understanding?

4. When people shower us with gifts or adoration because we are kind to them, what does Paul's and Barnabus's example show us to be the proper understanding and attitude?

5. What is the ultimate kindness of God that Barnabus, Paul, and you are all privileged to share far and wide?

6. What are the four specific instances of God's kindness toward the world?

7. Is the kindness of a joy-filled heart something you have ever asked God for?

Suggestions for Prayer:

1. Pray that you are a free channel for God's kindness when you minister to your prayer partner or to others.

2. Pray that you will be a witness to the Good News that Jesus died for the sins of the world, even for the sin of Adam from whom all sin, separation from God, and sickness including depression derives.

3. Pray for a joy filled heart.

→ **Day Two**

Scripture: Read Ephesians 4:26-32.

Questions for Meditation:

1. Anger seems to be the main topic of this scripture. Since anger is one of the symptoms of depression and is also an emotion that interferes with doing acts of kindness, please consider this devotion carefully. According to verse 26, is the emotion of anger a sin?

2. Why do you suppose it is so easy to let anger become sinful?

3. If you are feeling angry, should you isolate yourself from the person with whom you are angry, or does verse 26 suggest some action?

4. Does your anger ever result in "unwholesome talk"?

5. Are you willing to "appropriate" the gift of encouraging conversation for the building up of others?

6. How does anger grieve the Holy Spirit? Could it be because you are resisting the fruit He is seeking to build in you?

7. How might you get rid of all bitterness?

8. Have you been "kind and compassionate" to your prayer partner this week?

Suggestions for Prayer:

1. Thank God that even when you get angry and sin, He still loves you and the blood of Jesus was shed for just such sin as this.

2. Pray for boldness to reconcile with those with whom you are angry and bitter. Pray for a spirit of gentleness and forgiveness as you approach them.

3. Pray for forgiveness for the times you think you may have grieved the Holy Spirit. Thank God for His love, kindness, and mercy in forgiving you.

4. Pray that your faith might throw off all bitterness and then reach out and take hold of your new nature in Christ Jesus.

     Workbook: *Understanding Depression*, Turning Point, P. O. Box 22127, Chattanooga, TN 37422-2127

↪ **Day Three**

Scripture: Read Ruth 1:1-18.

Questions for Meditation:

1. This is one of the great stories of the Bible about kindness, commitment, and loyalty, all flowing from faith. Ruth, a gentile woman, had heard the word of the Lord from her mother-in-law, Naomi, and had believed. By faith, she appropriated God's own kindness, and it poured out willingly throughout her life. Do you think she ever had any regrets about showing kindness to Naomi even though she had to forsake everything to do so? If we truly allow God to build the pyramid of Christian character in our lives, do you think we would ever regret any of it?

2. That Naomi had discipled her daughters-in-law in godly kindness is revealed in what way at the time they left Moab?

3. What did Naomi say that revealed her knowledge of the source of true biblical kindness?

4. Does showing kindness require that one be able to see the outcome, to see the "payoff"?

5. While showing kindness, in what way did Naomi show her lack of trust in God's kindness toward her? Do you sometimes feel and speak with the same bitterness with which she spoke? Did God hold it against her?

6. Do you think it humanly possible to make the statement Ruth made to Naomi, "Where you go I will go, and where you stay I will stay. Your people will be my people and your God my God. Where you die I will die, and there I will be buried. May the LORD deal with me, be it ever so severely, if anything but death separates you and me" (verses 16-17).

Suggestions for Prayer:

1. Pray that you might show godly kindness to your prayer partner.

2. Pray that you might show godly kindness to your relatives, even those who are not blood relatives.

3. Pray for God's kindness toward yourself.

4. Thank Him for His kindness toward you.

Scripture: Read 2 Corinthians 6:4-10.

Questions for Meditation:

1. The Apostle Paul, though a murderous man in his early years and now having nothing of his own including family but only suffering and hardship, says of himself: "We commend ourselves in every way." From verse 4, what is it about his life that enables him to identify himself in this way?

2. Don't you have the same qualifications?

3. Verses 4-10 show a combination of hard experiences and good outcomes including the fruit of kindness which is our theme word this week. Can you see any similar connections in your life?

4. Romans 8:28 says "that in all things God works for the good of those who love him." Paul certainly learned this from his experience. How many things can you identify that God has worked together for good out of your hurts and sorrows?

Suggestions for Prayer:

1. Thank God for the righteousness He is working in your life.

2. Thank Him for your new identity, an identity which comes from Him and not from your past.

3. Thank Him for the kindness He is now building into your life.

4. Pray for your prayer partner that he or she will also identify with the new creation in Christ Jesus, the gift of God already given to both of you making you precious and loved offspring of the living God.

→ **Day Five**

Scripture: Read Galatians 5:22-23 and Colossians 3:12-14.

Questions for Meditation:

1. According to the Galatians passage, from where does kindness come?

2. What is a "fruit of the Spirit"?

3. How many of these fruits do you see forming in your life?

4. In Colossians 3:12, we see our theme word kindness again. From what you have learned over the past few weeks, how does one "clothe" themselves with these qualities?

5. According to verse 13, once we have clothed ourselves, what is the action that will appear in our lives? Have you done it?

6. In verse 14, Paul lists a final garment of clothing to be put on: love. This will be the theme element for next week. For now, meditate on the marvelous working of God in your life.

Suggestions for Prayer:

1. In any area where you do not see much of this fruit yet appearing, pray for yourself that the evil one cannot so accuse and convince you of failure that you are unable to see what God is doing.

2. Pray a prayer of appropriation, of putting on new "clothing" and thereby using your faith to reach out and take hold of these freely given fruits.

3. Pray for anyone for whom you might yet be having trouble forgiving.

4. Now, pray for yourself that you will have the power from God to forgive this person or persons.

5. Thank God for the gift of love which you will put on all the more beginning with the next meeting of the group.

Session **9**

Ministering to One Another in the Future

Meet With God

Personal Notes

Do the daily devotion each day (pages 94 to 95) prior to this group meeting.

Self-Awareness

Our weeks together as a group—and especially the "ministry to one another" process—have provided a valuable model for us as they help us understand what Christian community is all about. We've seen how caring brothers and sisters in Christ can minister to us—and how we, in turn, can reach out to others.

Have the other group members had a positive impact on your life? In what ways?

How did it make you feel to be on the "receiving end" of this ministry to one another?

How do you feel when God is able to use you in the lives of others?

This week we complete the building of our pyramid of new life according to the promise recorded in 2 Peter 1 by adding the ingredient of love. We add love and all of the other ingredients of our pyramid of life to the basic promise with which we began nine weeks ago:

Do we really believe
> **that our great God has granted through His Spirit**
> **everything we need to be happy and contributive**
> **as His children and servants?**
It's true!

Because depression causes people to feel very much unloved, we want to close our study by seeing in the Bible how desperately God loves each of us and how He has been at work in us to make us lovable.

Spiritual-Awareness

John 3:16
How does this loving act—God's giving His own Son—show a love that is different from human love?

This is our model of the kind of love that should be our goal. It is a sacrificial and self-giving love.

1 John 4:7-12
Where does this love come from?

Why are we to love others?

Galatians 2:20
What happens in our lives that enables us to show this supernatural love—love that goes far beyond what we are capable of in our own strength?

Romans 5:7-8
Do we deserve God's love toward us?

Do we love people because they deserve it?

What motivates our love?

1 Corinthians 13
This chapter tells us a great deal about love. What are some of the characteristics of a person who demonstrates *godly* love?

In this chapter we read about some spiritual gifts and such qualities as faith, generosity, even martyrdom. Then it says unless these qualities are based in *love*, they are nothing. Everything else, including our faith and hope, will one day pass away. (When we see the real thing in heaven, we won't need to have *faith* or to *hope* because then we can know and we can see.) But even then, love will continue to be at the center of our relationship with God and with our fellow believers.

Love is the finished product of our eight objectives. Let's return to our paraphrase version of 2 Peter 1 on page 10 and read it together beginning with Peter's greeting in verse 2. I hope that through the repetitions over these weeks, God has imprinted these words on your hearts.

This is how our faith grows beyond saving faith to become a way of life. I hope you'll return to these verses again and again in your personal study and let God remind you of what you've learned.

Workbook: *Understanding Depression,* Turning Point, P. O. Box 22127, Chattanooga, TN 37422-2127

As we come to our last time of application of the deep spiritual truths of God's Word, please remember that all of the new qualities of Christian faith that we have sought to put on each week and all the qualities of our old nature that we have worked to put off are all part of a lifelong process. What we have done is ask God to begin this life-changing process in us!

As kids grow up, good and effective parents ordinarily take care that they are fed nutritious food, get exercise and adequate sleep, and receive a good deal of ongoing family love. In the same way, as we grow up into the fullness of Christ Jesus, we too need a family to love us enough to see that we eat right spiritually and get spiritual exercise and rest.

The evil one will soon begin tempting you to believe that these weeks together were good for others in the group but that you were too far gone for even God to rescue. In order to see that this "father of lies" remains defeated in your lives, let's discuss some options for going on with God in the future.

One option would be to continue our prayer partner/mentor pairs and that we reduce our contacts to once a week except for emergency prayers in times of strong spiritual attack. Like everything else in this group, this is certainly your choice. Maybe you would like some time to pray and think it over before making a commitment.

Another option which could easily be an addition as well as an alternative to the first is to form an ongoing group which meets weekly with one of you as the facilitator. You could form around three ingredients: worship and prayer, Bible study, and ministry to one another. It wouldn't need to be as structured as our group here has been these past nine weeks, and the only preparation would be to choose the material for the Bible study. You already know how to support one another and how to carefront when the devil gets to roaring around.

Be prepared to give feedback about these options when the group meets. Perhaps you have some other ideas to suggest.

How do you feel about continuing the daily devotions which were designed especially for people struggling with depression? This week's devotions are especially recommended.

In addition to this week's daily devotions, please read the Bible verses at the end of Session Four again.

DAILY DEVOTIONS
Session Nine

This week, as in Session Four, our devotions consist simply of Bible verses selected to fill the heart, soul, and mind with truth from the Bible, truth that will push back the devil and his accusations. Remember to build your identity around these things and not around past experiences or feelings.

Look up each verse and meditate on it, perhaps also reading some of the verses before and after. Then pray whatever the Spirit puts on your heart in response to the truth of that verse.

→ **Day One**

1. Ephesians 2:20—I AM built on the foundation of the apostles and prophets with Christ Himself as the chief cornerstone.

2. 2 Peter 1:4 (from our theme passage)—I AM a participant in His divine nature.

3. Ephesians 2:10—I AM God's workmanship created in Christ Jesus to do good works.

4. Philippians 1:6—I AM confident of this: that He who began a good work in me will carry it on to completion.

5. 2 Corinthians 3:18—I AM being transformed into His likeness with ever-increasing glory.

→ **Day Two**

1. John 17:21-23—I AM one with my God and with my brothers and sisters in Christ.

2. 1 Corinthians 2:16—I HAVE the mind of Christ.

3. John 6:47—I HAVE everlasting life.

4. John 10:10—I HAVE life to the full (abundant life KJV).

→ **Day Three**

1. 1 John 5:4—I HAVE overcome the world.

2. Philippians 4:7—I HAVE the peace of God which transcends all understanding.

Workbook: *Understanding Depression*, Turning Point, P. O. Box 22127, Chattanooga, TN 37422-2127

3. Ephesians 2:18—I HAVE access to the Father by one Spirit.

4. Mark 16:17—I HAVE the power of Jesus' name to lay hands on the sick and see them recover, power against the enemy, and power to cast out demons.

→ Day Four

1. Philippians 4:13—I CAN do everything through Him who gives me strength.

2. 1 John 4:4—I AM from God and have overcome evil because the one who is in me is greater than the one who is in the world.

3. Philippians 3:14—I PRESS on toward the goal to win the prize for which God has called me heavenward in Christ Jesus.

4. Romans 8:2—I AM set free through Christ Jesus from the law of sin and death and have received the spirit of life.

→ Day Five

1. John 10:14-15—I KNOW that Jesus is my good shepherd; He knows me and laid down His life for me.

2. 2 Corinthians 2:14—I ALWAYS triumph in Christ.

3. 1 Peter 2:9—I AM part of a chosen people, a royal priesthood, a holy nation, a people belonging to God; and I may declare the praises of Him who called me out of darkness into His wonderful light.

4. Colossians 1:27—I SHARE in the glorious riches of this mystery which is Christ in me, the hope of glory.

References

Carson, Herbert M., *Depression in the Christian Family*, Evangelical Press, Phillipsburg, NJ, 1994.

Dayringer, Richard, Byron Eicher, Myron C Madden, John J. O'Hearne, *Dealing with Depression: Five Pastoral Interventions*, Haworth Press, Binghampton, NY, 1995.

Dravecky, Jan and Connie Neal, *A Joy I'd Never Known: One Woman's Triumph over Panic Attacks and Depression*, Zondervan Publishing House, Grand Rapids, 1998.

Hart, Archibald D., *Counseling the Depressed*, Dallas: Word, 1987.

Lowen, Alexander, M.D., *Depression and the Body: The Biological Basis of Faith and Reality*, Viking Press, New York, 1993.

Lloyd-Jones, Martyn D. *Spiritual Depression: Its Causes and Cure*, Wm. B. Erdmans, Grand Rapids, 1965.

Mondimore, Francis Mark, M.D., *Depression: The Mood Disease*, John Hopkins University Press, Baltimore 1993.

Norden, Michael J., M.D., *Beyond Prozac: Brain-Toxic Lifestyles, Natural Antidotes & New Generation Antidepressants*, Harper-Collins, Scranton, PA, 1995.

O'Connor, Richard, *Undoing Depression: What Therapy Doesn't Teach You and Medication Can't Give You*, Little Brown and Company, Boston, 1997.

Thompson, Tracy, *The Beast: A Journey Through Depression*, Plume, New York, 1996.

Yapko, Michael D., *Breaking the Patterns of Depression*, Doubleday, New York, 1997.

Workbook: *Understanding Depression*, Turning Point, P. O. Box 22127, Chattanooga, TN 37422-2127